The Fund Manager's
MARKETING
MANIFESTO

BEST PRACTICES FOR FUNDRAISING IN THE
ALTERNATIVE INVESTMENT INDUSTRY

Dennis Ford

BRIGHTON HOUSE
a s s o c i a t e s

PUBLISHED BY
Brighton House Associates
2 Park Central Drive, Suite 300
Southborough, MA 01772
www.brightonhouseassociates.com

Printed in the United States of America.

ISBN: 978-0-9829272-0-5

First Edition: 10 9 8 7 6 5 4 3 2 1

For information about special discounts or bulk purchases, please contact Brighton House Associates: 508-786-0480 or sales@brightonhouseassociates.com.

Publishing Consultant: Neuhaus Publishing (www.neuhauspublishing.com)
Cover Design: Red Door Media (www.reddoormedia.com)
Interior Design and Composition: Marian Hartsough Associates
  (www.marianhartsoughassociates.com)
Cartoonist: Ryan Hannus (hannusjobbus@gmail.com)

Table of Contents

Introduction

Most hedge fund managers today, regardless of their place in the market, are facing the same challenges: delivering performance, improving their dialogue with existing investors, and finding new investors. At the same time, many are still recovering from the 2008 financial crisis, when their assets dwindled not only because of market swings but also as a result of investor redemptions. They were dealt a double blow with both performance and assets under management hitting all-time lows.

In times past, investors stayed with funds through the inevitable ups and downs, often increasing their investments. In 2008, however, even stalwart, dependable investors left funds. This ushered in a new era. Today, fund managers must rethink how they go about communicating with and attracting investors.

Compounding the issue is a legal and regulatory landscape that continues to evolve and an institutional alternative investor community that is reevaluating investment strategies and reshuffling portfolios.

It may seem impossible to right the ship when everything's in flux, and many funds have closed as a result of the market dynamic. However, it is precisely times like these that present opportunities. And I firmly believe that the managers who take advantage of these opportunities will not only survive but also thrive.

So what should you do to improve your dialogue with current investors, find new ones, and ultimately, increase inflows? First, you must change your marketing strategy and tactics from inbound to outbound. There was a time when investors contacted fund managers, but that time has passed. You must actively reach out to investors and pursue allocations.

Second, you must market your fund constantly. Fundraising is not a one-time event. It must be an integral and ongoing part of your firm's effort to validate your model and ensure profitability and growth. Performance may still be king, but making connections and establishing relationships are a close second.

Third, you must adapt to the new time line. The allocation cycle used to be one to six months. Today it is typically nine to eighteen months, if not longer. This is a huge factor in the new fundraising equation. Adjust to it or be left behind.

Marketing is not an area most fund managers know much about. I've spoken with thousands of managers, and although some admit it more readily than others, it's clear that marketing is not their area of expertise—which is not surprising. But somehow, some way, you must have someone focus on marketing your funds. So the intent of this book is to help you grasp the basics and put in place the resources needed to make marketing part of the fabric of your firm.

Now, when I say someone, I do not mean just anyone. Successful fundraising requires a firmwide commitment, and it takes real leadership to get everyone in the entire firm, from the top to the bottom, to buy in. This person must take ownership of the process, communicate the importance of the effort up and down the ladder, and win everyone's support and participation. Then, he or she must guide the marketing effort.

"Guide" is the operative word. The chief marketer can't go it alone. His or her first step should be to assemble a SWAT team that can efficiently and effectively handle the numerous tasks and details that an ongoing marketing effort generates. Here's something to note: this team may not be your current team.

When the alternative investment world changed, so did the job descriptions of the investor relations and marketing staffs. Inbound and outbound are two distinct marketing styles. Each attracts certain personalities and requires special talents. It is imperative to adjust to the new paradigm if your firm is going to successfully raise capital.

Outbound and inbound marketing couldn't be more different. It is safe to say the two are like night and day. I will not go into all the subtle differences between them, but here's the core difference: the investor relations staff or marketers who used to screen incoming calls and identify the cream of the crop are not the folks to make the 30 to 50 outbound calls a day that are necessary to raise capital in this environment.

Inbound marketers are not familiar with the incredible effort it takes to vet a target list of investors. They don't know how to speak with cold prospects. They are not used to making 10 to 15 calls and receiving only one back. And they don't know how to set up conference calls and road trips with prospects.

When you have a team in place, then it's time to hone your branding and marketing message, prepare collateral materials that reflect your message and include critical investor information, and begin planning your marketing campaigns.

Your campaigns will be most successful if you pursue investors who are seeking your type of fund and strategy. When a firm's strategy fits an investor's search criteria, the connection is more likely to end in an allocation. It may seem like I'm stating the obvious, but the fact is that many managers contact investors for whom they are not a fit. The main reason? Bad and outdated investor data.

When faced with the prospect of raising capital, many managers buy a list of alternative investors. However, most of the databases that are on the market today are easily twelve to eighteen months out of date. Often they don't have current names and numbers, much less up-to-date search criteria. They have old information, which isn't useful considering the changes in the industry during the past few years.

Out-of-date data is responsible for many campaigns' poor results. It is also responsible for a lot of noise.

According to my back-of-the-napkin calculations, there are approximately 10,000 hedge funds, 5,000 private equity funds, 3,000 venture capital funds, and 2,000 real estate funds. There are also about 50,000 alternative institutional investors who fall into 16 categories, from small wealth advisors and family offices to large pensions, endowments, and corporations. The prevalence of poor quality databases in such a small industry means 20,000 fund managers are spamming 50,000 alternative investors. This has created a ton of needless noise in the market. Investors have told me that they receive hundreds of unsolicited phone calls, e-mails, and pitchbooks every week. As a result, they are having difficulty finding qualified managers who fit their search requirements. All that out-of-date data is creating gridlock.

So do yourself, investors, and the industry a favor: use fresh, current, and accurate investor information for your marketing campaigns.

Of course, ensuring that your data is of high quality is no easy task. And it's only one of hundreds you must tackle when planning and executing a continuous marketing effort—which is what gave me the idea for this book. There are many books already written on marketing. But because of the complexity and uniqueness of the alternative investment industry, managers, investor relations staff, and fund marketers need advice geared toward meeting their specific challenges.

To provide this insight, I asked several folks, each with a specific expertise, to help me write this book. The result is a collaboration that starts with the legal landscape and walks you through the process of creating collateral materials, launching a fundraising campaign, researching prospective investors, conducting e-mail and phone campaigns, organizing road trips, validating your fund's market position, devising a follow-up routine, and establishing a continuous dialogue with prospects and clients. These contributors are all experts in their niches, and their advice will help you adroitly market your fund in this new environment using the outbound marketing paradigm.

The game has changed, and it is incumbent on every manager who wants to raise capital to adjust to the new normal and have a marketing strategy in place. Using the strategies and techniques discussed in this book, you will be able to implement a sustained marketing effort that will be efficient and valuable to you, your prospects, and your investors.

The Preliminaries of a Fundraising Campaign

CHAPTER 1

The Legal Landscape

Peter D. Greene, Esq., Scott H. Moss, Esq., and Cole Beaubouef, Esq.

In January 2010, I was the keynote speaker at Jefferies Marketing Boot Camp in New York City. I spoke about the legal and regulatory parameters surrounding communication with prospective investors in the capital raising process. After my presentation, another speaker approached me. He introduced himself as Dennis Ford and told me he was putting together a book on marketing for hedge fund managers. However, there was a piece missing, he said. The book did not yet address the legal issues that hedge fund managers face in marketing their funds—precisely the issues I had talked about in my presentation. Dennis asked if I would consider turning my presentation into a chapter for his book.

Dennis was onto something. Working with fund managers day in and day out, I knew there was a real need for this type of information. The laws and regulations that apply to marketing a hedge fund always have been complex, and since the financial crisis, they have become even more important as capital raising has become more challenging. Just a few years ago, investors came to managers. Today, managers need to find investors, and as managers initiate investor conversations, they must be mindful of what they can and cannot say. The conse-quences of crossing the line are great, not only from a legal standpoint, but from a reputational one as well.

So, I agreed to contribute to Dennis's book and sought the help of Scott Moss and Cole Beaubouef. Scott and Cole also advise hedge fund managers, and Cole had worked with me on my presentation. I knew we all saw the need to provide managers with accessible explanations and practical advice. Together we could paint a picture of the legal landscape so managers were aware of the issues and prepared to dis-cuss them with their counsel.

Hedge fund managers are not unlike other businesses. Many have fewer than 20 employees, yet they manage substantial sums of money. They are in many ways small businesses, often started by one or two founders. Yet complexity underlies every aspect—from the technology they use to the transactions they conduct to the rules and regulations that govern them. Cole and I have seen firsthand how these dynamics, and their ever-changing nature, present unique challenges to fund man-agers, particularly when it comes to marketing. We also have seen how beneficial it is when managers have an understanding of the legal and regulatory issues, and work with a knowledgeable legal team. It not only gives a manager a better chance to comply with applicable law, but it increases the manager's credibility with prospective investors. After all, the culture of compliance at hedge funds is more important than ever.

Leo Burnett, the American advertising executive credited with creating the Jolly Green Giant, Toucan Sam, Charlie the Tuna, Tony the Tiger, and the Pillsbury Doughboy, is reported to have given the following tips related to marketing: "Make it simple. Make it memorable. Make it inviting to look at. Make it fun to read." Unfortunately, that advice does not work all that well for pooled private investments such as hedge funds, private equity funds, and venture capital funds. For man-agers or advisers of these investment vehicles, public statements are frowned upon and may even invite serious legal consequences. And yet the private fund industry, like any other industry, has products to sell and customers who are eager to buy. Unlike other industries, however, the restrictions on the manner of sale are significant, and the consequences of noncompliance—such as regulatory action and investor lawsuits—can be fatal, especially for start-up managers looking to grow their businesses.

In this chapter, we provide you with a brief overview of the more noteworthy legal and regulatory matters concerning pooled private-investment vehicles. The information we present is not intended to, nor does it, constitute legal advice. Rather, our purpose is to convey information that you should be aware of as you build your business. That is, this chapter should highlight important issues. The offering of interests in pooled private-investment vehicles is fraught with potential regulatory minefields. In addition, the laws and regulations surrounding such offerings are currently undergoing intense scrutiny by federal and state regulators, and very well may change. If you are contemplating, or in the process of, launching a fund, we advise you to seek appropriate legal counsel to discuss how these complex matters relate to your individual circumstances.

The Players

Although the private fund industry has often been described as "unregulated," an offering to investors of fund interests generally involves a complex web of statutory and other regulatory mandates on both the federal and state levels. This is because interests in a fund, such as those of a limited partnership or limited liability company, are considered securities. Two of the most important regulatory bodies monitoring the offering of fund interests are the Securities and Exchange Commission (SEC) and the Financial Industry Regulatory Authority (FINRA), formerly known as the National Association of Securities Dealers (NASD).

According to the SEC's website, its mission is "to protect investors, maintain fair, orderly, and efficient markets, and facilitate capital formation." To this end, the SEC is the primary regulator of not only the capital markets but also their participants, including managers of pooled private-investment vehicles. The SEC conducts its mission, in part, by working closely with other regulators, such as FINRA, and private sector actors, such as companies and individuals.

FINRA is a self-regulatory organization that operates under the auspices of the SEC. FINRA is responsible for the day-to-day supervision of brokers and dealers that are FINRA members. You should be aware of FINRA's broker registration requirements (and associated SEC regulations), because the marketing of fund interests may, absent an available exemption, require you, or the individuals you hire to market interests in your fund, to register as brokers. We explore this further in the section "Placement Agents and Consultants."

Fund Interests as Securities

Federal and state securities laws generally require that interests in a fund be registered as securities unless certain exemptions are available. Usually fund managers seek to avail themselves of these exemptions so they can avoid registering their fund interests as securities.

For pooled private-investment vehicles, the most common exemption managers seek is a private placement exemption, particularly the safe harbor provided by Rule 506 under Regulation D of the Securities Act of 1933. This exclusion provides that a fund's interests may be issued to an unlimited number of "accredited investors" and not more than 35 non-accredited investors, as long as certain solicitation requirements, among others, such as those precluding general solicitations or advertisements, are met.

Managers also avail themselves of exemptions under the Investment Company Act of 1940 (or the Company Act) which is enforced by the SEC and which imposes strict regulatory requirements (such as liquidity and disclosure restrictions) on registered investment companies. Section 3(c)(1) of the Company Act provides an exemption for funds that do not make public offerings of their securities and do not have more than 100 persons owning the fund's outstanding securities. The first portion of this exemption requires an examination of all of the facts and circumstances surrounding an offering. It also follows the general requirements of Regulation D outlined in the Securities Act and SEC guidance. The second portion of this exemption can be simultaneously easy (as in the case of counting individual investors in a fund) and difficult (as in the case of counting certain entity investors in a fund, such as funds of funds, and whether a manager must "look through" an entity investor to count the individuals who are invested in the entity).

The exclusion provided under Section 3(c)(7) of the Company Act allows a manager to have more than 100 investors participate in a fund without requiring registration as long as all such investors are considered "qualified purchasers" under the Company Act and the fund is not making a public offering of its securities. (The requirements for this portion of the exemption are the same as those contained in Section 3(c)(1) for a public offering.) A "qualified purchaser" is an investor who meets higher investment qualification standards than an accredited investor. Among certain other categories of potential investors, qualified purchasers are potential investors who own not less than $5 million in investments (such as securities or real estate), if an individual; own not less than $5 million in investments, if an entity; or invest, on a discretionary basis, not less that $25 million in investments for their own account or the accounts of other qualified purchasers.

You should seek the advice of counsel when examining the exclusions available under the Securities Act and the Company Act, as the penalties of noncompliance can be quite onerous.

Accredited and Non-Accredited Investors

Since most managers make fund offerings exclusively to accredited investors, this leads to the obvious question, what is an accredited investor? Generally, an accredited investor is an individual with a net worth, or combined net worth with his or her spouse, of $1 million, or a gross income during each of the past two calendar years that exceeds $200,000 (or $300,000 when combined with the annual income of his or her spouse). Additionally, institutional investors, such as corporations, partnerships, trusts, banks, savings and loan associations, insurance companies, and employee benefit plans may be accredited investors as long as certain dollar thresholds and other requirements are met. Accredited investors also include certain executive officers of a fund or of a fund's corporate general partner. For example, a president or vice president in charge of a particular business unit, or a director, may be an accredited investor even if that natural person does not satisfy the net worth or gross income thresholds noted above.

In addition to meeting the applicable dollar thresholds, potential investors also must be considered financially sophisticated, and their potential purchase of a fund interest must be considered a suitable investment. As part of the financial industry regulatory reform that was ushered in by the *Dodd-Frank Wall Street Reform and Consumer Protection Act of 2010*, signed by President Obama in July 2010, individuals are no longer entitled to include the value of their primary residence in their net worth in determining their status as an accredited investor. Likewise, the related amount of indebtedness secured by such person's primary residence up to its fair market value may be excluded when determining such person's net worth. However, indebtedness secured by the primary residence in excess of the value of the residence should be considered a liability and deducted from such person's net worth.

However, here's something important to note: even if you determine that a potential investor may be classified as an accredited investor, it is still possible that the investor will not be deemed qualified to invest in a particular fund. For instance, if a manager chooses to rely upon Section 3(c)(7) of the Company Act, it may necessitate heightened investor requirements, such as the qualified purchaser standard outlined earlier.

Many, if not most, fund managers limit offerings in their funds to accredited investors in order to avail themselves of the exemptions from securities registration requirements. However, as we mentioned, Rule 506 under Regulation D does provide that a limited number of non-accredited investors may participate in a Regulation D offering without implicating the need for registration. In order to accept such investors, however, fund managers are required to provide them with detailed disclosures about the operations of the fund, the fund manager, and the nature of the offering. Since these detailed requirements may be operationally difficult to compile, fund managers should consult with their legal counsel and carefully weigh the pros and cons of offering fund interests to non-accredited investors.

The Offering

In marketing the interests in your fund, you must not only determine whether prospects are accredited investors and otherwise financially sophisticated but also carefully scrutinize the manner in which prospects receive your materials and the information they contain. Failure to conduct a compliant offering process may cause you to lose the exemptions from registration provided by Regulation D and the Company Act.

The key here is to remember that the offering process must *not* be conducted via general solicitations or advertisements, including articles, notices, and other forms of communication in newspapers or magazines, or on television or radio. An offering also cannot be conducted at a seminar or meeting where the attendees are invited by general solicitation or advertisement. Can a manager give a TV or newspaper interview, or appear on a panel at an industry conference? Generally, the answer is yes. However, in doing so, can the manager discuss the particulars of his fund, such as the investment terms or track record? These issues are far thornier and only can be answered by a detailed review of the facts and circumstances surrounding the manager's activities.

In the past, the SEC has said that the requirements of Regulation D relating to general solicitations and advertisements could be satisfied if a manager had a preexisting relationship with a potential investor. This would allow a manager to form a "reasonable belief" that the potential investor would meet the eligibility standards imposed by Regulation D. Often, fund managers satisfy this condition by pointing to a prior business relationship (such as a past investment experience) with a potential investor. Fund managers often also may satisfy this condition by asking a potential investor to fill out a detailed questionnaire that gathers information about the investor's financial sophistication and liquidity.

The SEC also has provided some guidance to fund managers with past no-action letters. No-action letters are letters from SEC staff to individuals or firms who have requested clarification regarding whether their activities would be viewed as a violation of the federal securities laws. If after reviewing the facts and circumstances surrounding an activity, the SEC staff does not view the activity as a violation of the federal securities laws, it often provides a letter stating that it would not recommend that the SEC take any enforcement action against such persons or firms for such activity.

For instance, in a no-action letter to Woodtrails-Seattle, Ltd., dated August 9, 1982, the SEC stated that it would not take any enforcement action where a written offer was mailed to over 300 potential investors who previously had invested in limited partnerships sponsored by the manager, since the manager had a previous investment relationship with the investors.

In a no-action letter to Bateman Eichler, Hill Richards, Inc., dated December 3, 1985, the SEC stated that it would not take any enforcement action where a firm mailed a general letter to a select list of potential investors along with a detailed questionnaire that potential investors could complete, providing information about their financial condition and sophistication. Noting that the letter did not contain *any* specifics relating to the nature of the investment, and that no offering materials relating to the investment would be provided to the potential investors until their completed questionnaires were reviewed and their sophistication determined, the SEC stated that such a practice would not be viewed as a general solicitation and advertisement (and thus would not constitute a violation of Regulation D), provided that a substantive relationship was established between the time of the initial solicitation and the actual offer. The Bateman Eichler no-action letter provides important guidance for fund managers wishing to distinguish between any initial contact or solicitation of potential investors and actually engaging in an offering.

Technological advances over the past twenty years have added new wrinkles to the offering process. Although the Internet and other advancements in communication technology have in some ways made the marketing process more effective, they have also increased the chances of incurring regulatory scrutiny. As far back as 1995, the SEC was clear that the posting of information on a website may constitute a public offering of securities. Therefore, as with any other form of communication, fund managers must be aware of who has access to materials that are provided electronically. Password protection of an entire website—where a fund manager qualifies an investor as being accredited before granting him or her website access to its offering material—is the best practice. A bifurcated website, where part of the site is password protected and part is not, can be implemented, but it is tricky and should be fully vetted with counsel in advance.

The SEC also has used no-action letters to provide important guidance on offering processes conducted via electronic communications. In the case of Lamp Technologies, Inc., a website administrator sent general inquiries, along with detailed questionnaires, to potential investors. After the questionnaires were reviewed and the accredited investor status of the potential investors verified, the potential investors were provided a password to the firm's website so they could review offering materials for various funds. These potential investors also were precluded from investing in any of the funds on the website for a 30-day period after receiving the password. In a no-action letter dated May 29, 1997, the SEC stated that, on the basis of these restrictions, including the 30-day cooling-off period, the process through which these potential investors were introduced to fund investments would not be viewed as a general solicitation or advertisement.

In short, you should carefully analyze the methods and procedures you use to market interests in your fund to potential investors. Detailed compliance and record-keeping practices can protect you if you ever are placed under scrutiny for solicitation and offering practices. In fact, it is the offering process that often tests a manager's compliance and operational team. Fund managers are small businesses, and oftentimes their administrative infrastructure does not keep pace with the growth of assets under management. Many funds with strong performance records have failed because their compliance and operational teams were not sufficient to support their assets.

The Private Placement Memorandum

Although fund managers are not obligated by the Securities Act to provide any particular information to accredited investors, various federal and state anti-fraud provisions necessitate disclosure of certain details relating to the manager, the manager's fund, and the offering process. Disclosure is usually accomplished through a fund's confidential private placement memorandum (PPM). In general, the PPM should contain biographical information relating to key executives, such as their education, employment background, and investment expertise; detailed descriptions of a manager's investment strategy; potential conflicts of interest relating to the fund and its manager; and information about the risks of investing not only in the manager's fund but also in funds in general.

One key to producing an effective PPM is balancing full and fair disclosure of risks associated with a potential fund investment with any proprietary matters relating to a manager's investment strategy that a manager may wish to keep confidential. The reality is that the PPM is critically important. The PPM, if properly drafted, can and will help to protect the manager if an investor later brings any claims against the manager. Indeed, when managers faced major liquidity issues during the recent financial crisis, the provisions set forth in these documents—such as gates, suspensions, and side pockets—were critical to many funds' survival. Conversely, an improperly drafted PPM can hurt you if, for instance, it contains inaccurate or false disclosures.

You should be aware not only of the information set forth in the PPM but also the manner in which the PPM is distributed to potential investors. For example, are PPMs sequentially numbered? Does your staff note the date the PPM is sent to each potential investor and the dates of all follow-up conversations? Do you use restrictive legends in a fund's PPM to note that a potential investor may not disclose or distribute its contents to other persons, with the exception of his, her, or its professional advisers? Many managers take advantage of various software applications that help to ease these administrative tasks relating to the offering process.

Track Record and Performance

Quite often, a fund manager wishes to set itself apart from other managers by highlighting performance results. In fact, how to tout performance is near the top of the list of questions many attorneys get from clients. What is permissible is within the regulatory purview of the SEC.

Under Section 206 and Rule 206(4)-1 of the Investment Advisers Act of 1940 (or the Advisers Act), the SEC regulates all marketing materials used by investment advisers, which includes fund managers. Although many fund managers are not registered as investment advisers—there are several exemptions under the Advisers Act and state investment adviser regulations—their marketing materials are still subject to SEC oversight through the anti-fraud provisions of the Advisers Act.

Specifically, Section 206 of the Advisers Act, which applies to both registered and unregistered investment advisers, prohibits any fraudulent, deceptive, or manipulative activities by investment advisers (Rule 206(4)-8 under the Advisers Act contains an express prohibition against any fraudulent, deceptive, or manipulative activities, including making any untrue statement of material facts, by investment advisers with respect to investors in any pooled private investment vehicle managed by the adviser); Rule 206(4)-1 under the Advisers Act prohibits registered investment advisers from distributing any advertisement that contains any untrue statement or is otherwise false or misleading. Registered advisers also should be aware that Section 208 of the Advisers Act, among other things, prohibits stating or implying that the SEC or any other agency has sponsored or recommended the adviser by virtue of its registration.

The SEC is, of course, ever mindful of the manner in which fund managers portray past performance results in their disclosures to current and prospective investors. Through a series of SEC no-action letters and enforcement actions, the SEC has articulated several guidelines to aid fund managers who wish to disclose their recent track records. Performance is one of the regulatory areas in which the SEC has provided the most specific guidance.

One of the most influential SEC no-action letters addressing the area of performance disclosures was issued to Clover Capital Management, Inc., in 1986. Although the Clover letter does not provide a safe harbor for fund managers and is not considered to be an exhaustive list of prohibited practices, it does provide fund managers with detailed guidance for performance disclosures.

Regarding the presentation of model or actual performance results, the Clover letter establishes that the following omissions or practices would be considered misleading:

- The failure to disclose the effect of material market or economic conditions (this point is particularly important considering the recent market performance over the past two years)
- The failure to reflect the deduction of advisory fees, brokerage commissions, and other expenses that a client or fund paid or would have paid
- The failure to disclose whether and to what extent the results portrayed include the reinvestment of dividends and other earnings
- The suggestion of potential profits without also disclosing the possibility of potential losses
- The comparison of results to an index without disclosing all material factors relevant to the comparison
- The failure to disclose any material conditions, objectives, or investment strategies used to obtain the performance

The Clover letter notes also that the following omissions or practices would be considered misleading in the presentation of model performance results:

- The failure to disclose prominently the limitations inherent in model results
- The failure to disclose, if applicable, any material changes in investment strategy of the model portfolio during the period, and the effect such changes would have had on the model portfolio
- The failure to disclose, if applicable, that some of the securities or strategies inherent in the model portfolio do not relate, or relate only partially, to the *current* services offered by the manager
- The failure to disclose, if applicable, that the manager's clients had investment results that were materially different from the results of the model portfolio

The SEC noted also that if actual performance results are only for a select group of clients, failure to disclose the basis on which the selection was made and the effect of the practice on the results would be misleading. Cherry picking—whether with respect to classes of shares, series of shares, or particular investments—is always problematic.

Finally, the Clover letter noted that whether any particular disclosure relating to performance results would be considered false or misleading depends upon the overall facts and circumstances surrounding the disclosure. The SEC noted specifically that it would review the form and content of the disclosure, the implications or inferences arising out of the disclosure, and the sophistication of the prospective client or investor before ruling.

In 2008, the SEC provided additional commentary relating to past performance. Specifically, in a no-action letter to TCW Group, Inc., the SEC permitted an investment adviser to distribute marketing materials that identified not less than five holdings that contributed to the positive performance of an account, as long as such holdings were accompanied by an equal number of holdings that contributed to the negative performance of the account.

Transparency

An additional issue that you should be aware of during the marketing process is side letters. Frequently, managers use side letters to give some investors better terms or more transparency. Although side letters are not prohibited by any federal or state securities laws and may be beneficial, particularly in attracting seed capital during a fund's start-up phase, the SEC has commented that they are troubling because they afford some investors a potential advantage over others. For example, an investor who has full access to a fund's portfolio holdings (when other investors do not) is potentially able to make a decision to redeem in advance of another investor due to increased knowledge of the fund's holdings. If this access is coupled with increased liquidity, the unequal treatment of investors becomes even more troubling.

The inequality of information is something about which you should be very careful. If you sign a side letter providing more transparency or portfolio access to one investor, strongly consider giving that right to everyone. Managers contemplating the use of side letters also should obtain the advice of counsel.

Placement Agents and Consultants

Launching and growing a fund is a full-time entrepreneurial endeavor. Managers, of course, are generally consumed with creating and building a performance track record, and therefore often require the assistance of third parties to market their funds. In this respect, you will be pleased to know that there is a well-developed industry specializing in assisting with marketing efforts. However, you also should be aware that taking advantage of these services may raise certain regulatory concerns. Since a fund's interests are considered securities under federal and state securities laws, there is a distinct possibility that anyone effecting transactions relating to those interests, including third-party marketers, will fall under regulatory scrutiny. Of particular concern are certain requirements relating to brokers imposed by the Securities Exchange Act of 1934 (or the Exchange Act) and various regulatory restrictions imposed by FINRA.

Under the Exchange Act, it is generally unlawful for any person "to effect any transaction in, or to induce or attempt to induce the purchase or sale, of any security" unless such person is registered with the SEC as a broker or dealer. The Exchange Act generally defines a broker as any person who, for compensation, is engaged in the business of effecting transactions in securities for the accounts of others.

A fund as an issuer does not act as a broker since it does not effect transactions for the accounts of others, only itself. There are exemptions from the registration requirements for certain employees of a manager who are involved in the offering process (however, managers should be careful to consult counsel on the availability of these exemptions). However, when a fund manager engages a third party to assist in the solicitation process and, in particular, if the third party is paid a commission based on, for example, the number of investors it brings to a fund or the amount of capital allocated by each investor it brings to a fund, the third party generally will need to be registered as a broker.

Some third parties provide, or purport to provide, limited "consulting" advice to fund managers regarding solicitation of potential investors. These "finders" claim that because they are not engaged in securities transactions, they need not register as brokers. You should note, however, that this finder exemption is construed narrowly. To the extent that a "finder" is involved in the negotiation process for the sale of fund interests or to the extent that the finder receives any transaction-based compensation, registration as a broker may be required. Unregistered third-party marketers who act as brokers open fund managers to legal and reputational risk. These marketers also give investors who purchase interests on the basis of their activities a right to rescission of their investment in the fund if the marketers are found to have violated securities laws in connection with the offering.

Registered investment advisers have additional regulatory concerns to keep in mind when utilizing the services of a third-party marketer.

However, if you, like many fund managers, are an unregistered investment adviser, you should still be mindful of these issues and consider them as part of your best practices.

Specifically, any person, including a broker, who refers investors to a registered investment adviser may be deemed a solicitor and be subject to certain regulations under the Advisers Act (Rule 206(4)-3). These regulations, commonly referred to as the "cash solicitation rule," provide that it is unlawful for any registered investment adviser to pay a cash fee to a solicitor for solicitation activities unless certain requirements are met. Judicial interpretations and subsequent SEC commentary have clarified that the requirements of the cash solicitation rule do not apply to cash payments by registered investment advisers to individuals or companies solely to compensate that individual or company for soliciting investors to a pooled investment vehicle managed by the adviser. However, as best practices, many advisers, both registered and unregistered, follow the requirements of the cash solicitation rule. Among other items, the cash solicitation rule requires the following:

- The solicitor must not fall into certain "bad boy" categories, for example, having past criminal convictions
- The cash fee paid to a solicitor must be paid pursuant to a written solicitation agreement to which the adviser is a party
- Adequate disclosure regarding the solicitation activities must be made to an adviser's client or, in the case of an adviser to a pooled investment vehicle, the pool's investors

For third-party solicitors, the written solicitation agreement must:

- Describe the solicitation activities and the compensation to be received
- Contain a representation that the solicitor will perform its duties in a manner consistent with the directions of the adviser and consistent with the requirements of the Advisers Act

- Require the solicitor to provide the client, or in the case of an adviser to a pooled investment vehicle, the pool's investors, with a current copy of the adviser's brochure or other disclosure document, such as Part II of its Form ADV.

It is important to note that, due to recent scandals relating to the investment with fund managers of public pension funds, so-called "pay-to-play" regulations have become a prime area for regulatory scrutiny and action. For instance, certain state legislators (such as those in New York) have banned the use of third-party marketers by hedge funds for soliciting public pension-fund investments. Additionally, the SEC also has recently passed certain restrictions that will, as of September 2010, affect the use of third-party marketers by fund managers to solicit government clients. Briefly, the new SEC rule will require such marketers to be registered as brokers or investment advisers.

The adviser registration issue also has been front and center of various legislative proposals that have been discussed on both the federal and state levels during the past year. As a result of the Dodd-Frank Act mentioned earlier, many previously unregistered fund managers will be forced to register as investment advisers at the federal level if they manage assets in excess of $150 million. It is also anticipated that state registration requirements will undergo significant revisions in the near future.

Under the current regulatory regime, which will remain in place until July 2011, an investment manager is exempt from registration as an investment adviser if he has fewer than 15 clients, does not advise a company registered under the Company Act, and does not hold himself out to the public as an investment adviser. Like the general solicitation and advertisement restrictions imposed by the Securities Act with respect to the fund interests themselves, these prohibitions mean that an unregistered fund manager must be careful how he portrays his business to the public so as not to run afoul of the exemption. The Advisers Act does, however, provide that a fund manager will not be considered in violation of the restriction by conducting a non-public offering of privately placed fund interests pursuant to securities laws, because the manager is not holding himself out to the public. Although registered investment advisers need not concern themselves with this holding-out restriction, these advisers nonetheless must be cognizant of the general solicitation and advertising restrictions imposed by the Securities Act.

Summary

In closing, we thought it would be helpful to provide some key points to remember as you build your business:

- Do not overstate or understate the facts relating to your business. Provide investors and potential investors with a realistic and fair presentation of the fund you are marketing. If the fund is a worthwhile investment, data presented in an even-handed manner will reflect this.

- They say that sunlight is the best disinfectant, and oftentimes full and fair disclosure of material facts to investors can prevent allegations of violations of a fund manager's fiduciary duties down the road. Err on the side of too much disclosure.

- Be aware of the best practices relating to your business. Even if not legally required, such practices can be used as a marketing tool and are increasingly being demanded by both institutional and individual investors.

- Relationships with third-party marketers can help your business succeed, but be mindful that such relationships should be expressly addressed in a written contract with appropriately registered persons.

- Stay apprised of the most current legal and regulatory developments, particularly in the current economic environment. As members of an industry that is currently in the regulatory spotlight, these developments can dramatically impact your relationships with current and potential investors.

- Finally, no matter how modest or large your business, and no matter what type of legal and compliance staff you may have, remember that the culture of compliance starts at the top. All members of your staff, including senior executives, should familiarize themselves with the rules and regulations that limit communications with investors. The penalties for violating these rules, including possible FINRA sanctions and SEC investigations, are far too significant to ignore.

Other than generating alpha, marketing is perhaps the most important aspect of our industry. Without capital, there is no business. Although the necessity of customers may be less obvious for hedge funds than it is for retailers, manufacturers, doctors, lawyers, and accountants, it is no less critical. Because our space centers around accepting capital from investors, it is highly regulated. It is so important—especially in our new world order—to carefully monitor marketing practices to ensure compliance with the letter and spirit of the law. Completeness and accuracy always should be your guideposts with respect to disclosure. Make sure you tell investors the full story and the true story. Failure to do so eventually will come back to harm you.

PETER D. GREENE is Vice Chair of Lowenstein Sandler's Investment Management Group as well as a member of the firm's Corporate Department. Peter is familiar with all aspects of operating the business of a hedge fund and its investment management-related entities, including the formation and launch of investment funds, the formation of management entities, compliance, trading, investor relations, fund audits, fund administration, third-party marketing, employment, and executive compensation. Peter also has particular experience with the hedge fund restructurings that have become so commonplace since late 2008. From 2000 to 2002, Peter was the General Counsel and Chief Operating Officer at an investment manager responsible for the man-

agement of a $600 million family of funds specializing in Private Investments in Public Equities (PIPEs).

SCOTT H. MOSS is a member of Lowenstein Sandler's Corporate Department and a member of the Investment Management Group, as well as a member of the firm's M&A and Corporate Finance Practice Group. Scott's practice includes the formation of investment funds, investment adviser regulation, broker-dealer regulation, and compliance. Scott also has experience in corporate matters, business planning, securities regulation, mergers and acquisitions, and banking and finance.

COLE BEAUBOUEF is an associate in Lowenstein Sandler's Investment Management Group, as well as the firm's Corporate Department. His practice includes structuring and forming private funds and managed accounts with various investment strategies, investment adviser regulation and compliance, and advising on regulatory and compliance matters relating to commodity pool operators and commodity trading advisors.

CHAPTER 2

Persuasive Marketing Collateral Wins Investor Attention

Ann Trautenberg

In 2008, I, like most people, watched the financial crisis unfold with amazement. And like most people, I couldn't hazard a guess as to where it would all lead. However, being an experienced marketer, I knew this: for firms to recover, it was going to take a lot of hard work—hard marketing work. I also knew that my company's skill set could complement and augment the new fundraising initiatives that inevitably would come about as part of the recovery from the economic downturn.

During my days at Forrester Research, a premier research, marketing, and consulting company where I worked prior to starting Boston Consulting Partners, I often consulted with firms in the financial industry. Consequently, I had a solid network of contacts to tap and could map out how BCP could move into the alternative arena.

As I reached out, many of my contacts confirmed our direction. Fund managers, in particular, frequently commented that of all the industries or sectors hurt by the debacle, they anticipated the alternative investment space would have the most difficulty recovering. The reason? There was a distinct lack of marketing knowledge, skills, and resources in the alternative space.

Funds with less than $200 million under management usually have only three or four employees, and rarely invest in a full-time marketer. Funds with $200 million to $1 billion in assets can have as few as six to twelve employees, one of whom is a marketer or investor relations staff. Contrasting this with other industries in which a $500 million company has a vice president or director who is responsible for a full marketing staff or department, I could see that there was a void in the alternative arena that BCP could fill.

In addition to lacking internal resources, there were few external resources these firms could really rely on. There were firms that specialized in design, branding, or advertising, but there were few that not only provided strategic and tactical expertise but also understood this market. The general consensus was that by lacking marketing resources, these funds would be at a disadvantage as the economy pulled out of the recession.

Prior to 2008, most investors contacted fund managers, so marketing expertise wasn't critical to building a successful fund. Going forward, however, fund managers would need to have outbound marketing campaigns to raise money. Compounding their lack of expertise would be the lack of high-level marketing consultants who could help them learn the nuances of proactive fundraising.

It was in response to this need that BCP expanded into the alternative arena. As a full-service marketing firm, we work with fund clients on positioning, branding, designing, and most important, generating compelling content and a precise marketing message. Because of our backgrounds in marketing, and an in-depth understanding of the alternative investment industry, we can create top-notch cohesive and professional marketing materials.

The economic recovery is not going to be quick or easy. But more important, the fundraising environment has changed. Specifically, the time investors take to make allocations is longer (nine to eighteen months) and they have added a rigorous review of the management team. Investors are now wiser and more demanding. If fund managers are going to secure allocations, they have to adjust. From our experience, we know that one of the first steps managers should take is to fine-tune their branding, messaging, and marketing collateral.

Investors today are bombarded with marketing materials. On a weekly basis, a typical investor receives hundreds of e-mails, tear sheets, and brochures from alternative fund managers vying for his or her attention. The fact is that the financial crisis of the past few years has left institutions with fewer dollars to invest, and the competition for a smaller pot is fierce. Attracting investors is not as easy as it once was.

Adding to the difficulty is a change in investors' requirements. Outstanding performance is no longer their only criterion. Being an exceptional money manager is certainly important, but at this juncture, there are plenty of firms that have strong track records.

To win allocations in this environment, you must stand out from the competition in more ways than one—and the first way is to have top-notch marketing collateral. You must provide potential investors with high-quality, professional materials. Materials that engage them, communicate clearly and concisely, and present the information they want to see in a way that helps them to decide quickly and easily if you are a potential fit for their needs.

Often investors find fund materials inscrutable and lacking. It is common to find pages and pages of wordy explanations that don't include important information. The all-important graphical representation of data and performance can't be deciphered, and crucial data is omitted. Add in distracting random logos, colors, and layouts and investors simply can't understand the message. They also have no time and even less patience to try to deduce it.

To raise capital, it's imperative that your materials engage and compel investors to read on. Simply put, if you can't entice investors to read your materials, you surely won't win their business.

Marketing Materials

So what marketing materials are required to fundraise successfully? At a minimum, you need to prepare the following four items:

- A tear sheet
- A pitchbook
- Monthly and quarterly reports
- A due diligence questionnaire

To secure allocations in this competitive market, fund managers must be more effective at every juncture of the marketing process. This requires investing in every piece of collateral that they put in front of prospects.

Before we go any further, you should note that all marketing materials—including tear sheets, pitchbooks, reports, and DDQs—must be reviewed and approved by your legal team prior to distribution. Addressing legal and compliance issues, and including appropriate disclaimers, is critical before distributing to investors.

A Tear Sheet

A tear sheet is your first written opportunity to market your firm. A superior tear sheet grabs investors' attention and compels them to investigate further. It is a teaser, and the one chance you have to make the first cut. If you don't grab their interest here, you'll never get to the next step.

Investors know what they want to see at this point. Depending on the type of fund, trading strategy, and track record, they expect certain information and data, and a particular format and flow. They also prefer fund managers to provide performance snapshots using certain types of tables and charts. If your materials don't conform to their expectations, you can easily be disqualified.

The typical length of a tear sheet is one to two pages. The most impressive tear sheets immediately give insight into a firm's unique value. They also quickly communicate—ideally in a few sentences and at most a paragraph or two—why an investor should continue reading. If your tear sheet fails to do this, right into the circular file it will go.

A tear sheet highlights key data and information. That is, all the quick facts associated with your fund, such as fund terms, performance, and service providers. Leave out critical elements—or, conversely, include unnecessary information—and you could miss your opportunity. Remember, the point of a tear sheet is to showcase your firm and whet investors' appetites.

Here's a case in point. Recently, we visited with an institutional investor who oversees a multibillion-dollar portfolio. We asked what materials he's received that he would consider good. He reached for a stack of materials from that day's mail and began leafing through. More than 40 funds had sent him their literature and he found only one tear sheet that grabbed his attention. The others he tossed. There were more in his e-mail inbox, but he said the results would be no different.

What made that one tear sheet stand out? According to the investor, it was clean, crisp, and to the point. In two pages, it clearly conveyed the fund's strategy, performance, background, and terms—all the things he needed to know to decide his next step. Its professional appearance also gave him a favorable impression of the firm.

A Pitchbook

Presenting your firm's pitchbook is typically the second opportunity you have to explain your fund's positioning to a potential investor after an initial introduction. Pitchbooks provide more in-depth information and data about your firm, and can help solidify an investor's interest.

A big mistake many fund managers make is thinking that "in-depth" means "long." Potential investors will not read a 35- or 50-page pitchbook, much less one that's 75 pages. Remember, at this stage they are evaluating numerous firms for a potential fit. They know that the length and weight of this document do not necessarily equate to a better investment. If anything, an overly long pitchbook implies that the manager did not take the time to cull the information to provide only that which is most relevant, useful, and instructive.

The most effective pitchbooks are ideally 15 pages and at most 25. They have a distinct best-practices flow, so investors receive the information they want sequenced in an order that's easy to absorb. Too often, managers incorrectly assume that investors care only about the data and not the way it is presented.

When creating a quality pitchbook, there are several decisions you must make, including how you write your introduction, discuss the firm's infrastructure, articulate the fund's performance, and highlight the details that differentiate your firm from the competition. You also must determine how to highlight information using the most effective visuals. The choices you make represent your firm to an investor and can make or break your opportunity.

Monthly and Quarterly Reports

Current investors and prospects have an intense interest in following and understanding your fund. In particular, potential investors want to monitor your fund's performance for a number of months before making an allocation.

Your ability to clearly and succinctly deliver this information in a timely manner is critical. In fact, many managers have started to document their monthly and quarterly performance in two- to five-page reports as a key part of their marketing process. They recognize the need to invest time and money in these reports.

Monthly and quarterly reports provide an opportunity for managers to connect with potential investors and demonstrate their ability to provide the ongoing communication and transparency investors want to stay informed. It is also an opportunity to maintain a dialogue and relationship with existing investors. Informed investors tend to be more comfortable with their investments and less likely to request redemptions.

So what do prospects want to see in your reports? Performance is a must. If your fund underperforms, investors want to understand why and how you will address that going forward. If your fund met its goal or outperformed, investors want to know how you intend to leverage your success. Additionally, investors are interested in investment news, market viewpoints or opinions, and data analysis. Providing reports that are valuable, thought-provoking, and relevant is the recipe for attracting and keeping an audience.

As you create your materials, keep in mind that what works in one medium doesn't always work in another. For example, a design that makes information easy to follow in print may not do so when converted to electronic format. Yet fund managers must communicate with their audience using multiple mediums. Rather than produce more than one set of materials—an unnecessary expenditure of time and money—create materials that are effective whether they are distributed electronically or in hard copy.

The Due Diligence Questionnaire

A piece in the marketing process that often is not given the attention it deserves and requires is the due diligence questionnaire, or DDQ. The DDQ is not a marketing-focused document. Rather, it is a list of questions and answers about the fund prepared by the principals and their legal counsel. Nevertheless, it should have the same look and feel as the rest of your marketing materials.

When investors ask for a fund's DDQ, they are looking for detailed information, and your responses must be written clearly and concisely. Among other things, the DDQ generally provides investors with information about how your fund operates, the regulatory authorities with which it is registered, and the principals of the firm and any potential conflicts of interest. In essence, it provides a snapshot of the operational, legal, financial, and other aspects of your business. Your answers also elucidate how your firm makes all these functions work together as a coherent unit.

A fund manager who has done a great job with his or her tear sheet, pitchbook, and monthly or quarterly reports can still fail to make the investor's short list if he or she doesn't understand the real purpose and value of the DDQ and give it proper attention. The way you prepare the DDQ may determine whether or not a potential investor proceeds with the due diligence process.

Branding Your Firm

Having a clear and consistent identity and message—or brand—that differentiates you from your competition is critical to establishing a leadership position.

Many alternative fund managers think that only consumer goods companies such as Pepsi or Lexus must invest in branding. The reality is that branding is equally important in the business-to-business and financial worlds. Although you're communicating with a small and highly educated audience, branding influences the choices they make. Your branding projects an image in the marketplace that is paramount in creating a comfort level for investors today and for years to come.

Your brand identity and message should be showcased in your tear sheet, pitchbook, quarterly and monthly reports, and all other communications materials that are part of your outbound marketing campaign. (In this chapter, we focus on the minimum materials you need to launch a capital-raising campaign. However, there are many others, such as brochures, websites, and newsletters, which can enhance the marketing process.)

Implementing your identity and message consistently across all written materials is key to building a brand that has positive associations in the marketplace and enhances your firm's reputation over time. This is true for all alternative fund managers, from the neophyte to the highly experienced. Investors look for managers with excellent reputations. How does an alternative fund manager build this reputation? Branding.

Developing Your Logo

All top investment firms spend substantial time, money, and effort finding a design firm that will create the perfect branding identity, or logo. A logo may seem like a trivial issue, but it's an opportunity for you to create an image in an investor's mind.

The goal of logo development is to create a compelling, relevant, and current symbol that investors associate with your offering. Think of the Mercedes logo or that of BMW or Lexus. Those images conjure up feelings and judgments. The same applies to your logo as it relates to your fund.

Many fund managers make the rookie mistake of choosing a logo based on something they like or for which one of the founders has affection. The associations those symbols may elicit for investor audiences may be drastically different—and potentially a hindrance. Your company's logo is a visual representation of your brand, and it can affect the image and the message you are trying to project to the marketplace.

It is important not to be frivolous or cavalier when choosing a logo. To the contrary, it is imperative that you give your logo design a lot of thought and consideration. You must take the time to consider what differentiates your company from competitors, what values you hold, and what message you are trying to send. If you take the time to think through these questions, you'll be able to develop a logo that is a strong and simple representation of the image you are striving to achieve in the marketplace.

Creating a Look and Feel

Times change. What's in one year may be out the next. Every decade has its own look and feel when it comes to marketing. If you want your company to be both distinctive and current, you have to be aware of the critical look-and-feel do's and don'ts when creating your brand.

The look and feel of a brand includes the logo, colors, layout, typography—even the graphs and charts. In short, everything you use to represent your company's image and information is part of its look and feel. Leaders in winning marketing teams work daily to create and maintain an image that is crisp, clean, and always up-to-date.

Potential investors see the marketing materials of hundreds of firms that are competing against yours to win allocations. These investors are judging your firm relative to its peers as they read your marketing materials. Some are conscious judgments—and some are not.

It is imperative, therefore, to know what works and what doesn't, as well as what's new and current versus what's old and out of date.

It's important to incorporate design elements that other fund managers are using to communicate complex investing strategies and make them easily understood. For example, I am frequently asked if charts and graphs should be three dimensional and if stock photography is acceptable. Such decisions may seem insignificant, but in fact they can impact an investor's decision.

If your materials follow the principles of branding, an investor will be able to pick up your tear sheet, pitchbook, monthly and quarterly reports—in essence, anything that your firm produces—and know it's from your firm without even seeing the company name.

Budgeting for Success

To successfully fundraise, it is imperative that you make the necessary commitments right from the start. Creating effective marketing materials requires not only a time commitment but also a financial one. Let's not mince any words here; your marketing collateral is one of the first items you must complete in order to launch a successful fundraising campaign.

Many investors tell us they are frustrated. Fund managers contact them regularly hoping to secure millions in allocations and yet they haven't invested in their own marketing communications materials. What conclusion do these investors draw? That these fund managers don't take the due diligence process seriously.

Marketing materials created by professional firms stand out. They look different, read differently, and elicit a different response. They also make an investor's job easier, primarily because they are created with his or her needs in mind.

By making a financial investment in your materials and hiring a professional firm that has the expertise to create them, you let prospective investors know that their time and consideration are important to you. You send the message that you are making the effort to put your best foot forward and doing the work necessary to make your information clear and direct.

It's tempting to create marketing materials in-house. After all, who knows more about your business than you? But before you do, consider this: every day, we talk with fund managers who thought the same thing. They are being paid high salaries based on fund performance and are frustrated because they are spending days, weeks, and even months not only creating materials but also often recreating them based upon feedback from prime brokers, investors, and others. Not only would their time be better spent doing what they do best, but in the end they aren't confident their materials are suitable for their market.

So what does it cost to have a marketing company create high-quality materials with cogent and compelling content?

Prices vary fund to fund, depending upon the complexity of the firm, its trading strategies, audience, and other factors. Your branding requirements will also affect the cost. However, a quality firm can provide a detailed price quote for each deliverable. Typically, firms quoting at the low end use templates and create very little original content, leaving that to you. Estimates at the high end usually include custom content and custom graphic design.

Note that cost estimates should always be vetted and thoroughly understood. Firms you are considering should not quote a flat fee without spending time with you to understand your firm, your strategy, and your unique value. Estimates should always be based upon your firm's specific situation and needs. That said, here are some general guidelines.

Marketing Materials	Graphic Design Outsourced, Content Generated In-house	Graphic Design and Content Outsourced	Estimated Hours
Tear sheet	$1,000 – $2,000	$3,500 – $5,000	30 – 40
Pitchbook	$10,000 – $15,000	$20,000 – $25,000	80 – 100
Monthly and quarterly reports	$1,000 – $2,000	$3,500 – $5,000	30 – 60

It is clear from these very general guidelines that to outsource your initial marketing materials, you have to budget a minimum of approximately $25,000. Most firms should allocate $35,000 to $50,000 because of ongoing revisions and updates. If you have a complex offering, you may have to spend much more.

If you're still not convinced of the value of outsourcing this effort, do a cost-benefit analysis. Do you think you and your in-house staff can write and refine a tear sheet in less than 40 hours? A pitchbook in less than 100 hours? If so, will the content be of professional quality? Will the materials be as effective as they could be? And what other important tasks will not be getting done while you and your staff focus on creating these materials?

Your marketing and investor relations staff should be taking care of clients and creating investor inflow potential. BCP has observed first hand that taking six weeks to create marketing collateral could be better spent. Unfortunately, these are the hard facts that are lost on most inexperienced marketers.

We have calculated that as a general rule of thumb, an in-house marketing executive's time and pay to generate the content and manage an outside design firm costs about $50,000 and takes approximately six weeks. Using a full-service marketing firm costs roughly $35,000 and still takes the same amount of time *except that it usually requires only one week of the in-house manager's time.* $50,000 or $35,000? Six weeks or one week? Do your own analysis, but we think you'll find that it pays to hire a full-service marketing firm.

Here's another, simpler way to look at it: you need only to receive an investment of $1 million to cover the costs.

Professional Marketing Firms

There are four main types of firms that offer marketing support to alternative fund managers:

- Graphic design
- Branding and advertising
- Content creation

- Specialized outsourced marketing

The challenge in choosing a firm is determining your needs and finding the best fit.

Graphic Design Firms

Many fund managers engage graphic design firms anticipating that they will create compelling content as well as a stunning design. Don't assume. Ask up front if a firm writes content and if they have experience in your particular area.

Graphic design firms create the look and feel of collateral materials. Typically they don't understand the nuances of the alternative investment industry or your target audience. They don't have the background or knowledge to write the content required to make an impact, nor do they know which graphs, charts, or diagrams will provide the best representation of your firm and strategy.

If you have written content, however, and you have already established the charts, graphs, or diagrams you want to use, there is an abundance of graphic design firms that can take your information and create templates for tear sheets, pitchbooks, monthly and quarterly reports, and so on.

A top quality design firm should be able to produce attractive charts, graphs, and slides. That said, since good design is subjective, it is important to see relevant samples to ensure the design firm can deliver a product that aligns with your vision and differentiates your firm and your fund in the marketplace. A firm may say they can meet your expectations, but if you haven't seen samples, you could be sorely disappointed.

When we searched for top designers, we interviewed nearly 50 people before finding the talent that could create the quality designs and look and feel we were comfortable delivering to our clients.

Branding and Advertising Firms

There are many types of branding and advertising firms that are experts at creating marketing materials. When you delve deeper, however, the majority of these companies are specialists in particular industries. You rarely find firms that specialize in financial services, and fewer still in the niche comprising alternative investments. As a result, branding and advertising companies rarely understand your target audience or the best way to influence it. The basic advertising principles that drive consumer or even business-to-business marketing don't work in the alternative investment industry and, in some cases, can't be applied because of government regulations.

Content Creation Firms

Content creation firms help you refine your message and then write content. Usually these firms are divisions of larger branding and advertising firms and have professional writers and marketers on staff who have extensive knowledge of marketing's best practices. They generally have experience in many industries—except alternative investments.

However, the alternative investment industry is not only different from any other but also quite complex. To create marketing materials, writers need knowledge of investments and investment strategies, markets, fund structures, SEC and FINRA guidelines, historical challenges, investor attitudes and motivations, and more.

Unlike many other industries where you can apply the same principles to achieve the same results, this industry is fraught with nuances that create obstacles for firms attempting to provide services to fund managers. Typically content creation firms promise results, but they don't know what they don't know. As a result, the fund manager ends up frustrated at the inability of the firm to articulate the differentiators of their firm, strategy, or trading process.

The best choice is to find a firm that has a team of experienced writers, consultants, and analysts that have industry experience, background, and knowledge. These executives will be able to ask you the right questions that enable them to extract important data. Then they leverage their writing and communication skills to deliver a document that informs the reader with the information you want to relay.

Specialized Outsourced Marketing Firms

When embarking on an effort to create an engaging, persuasive, and successful arsenal of marketing materials, it is ideal to work with a firm with expertise in the alternative investment industry, a background in marketing, and knowledge of investors' needs—what they need to see and what they don't. There are many companies offering individual services to fund managers, but only specialized marketing firms offer strategic *and* tactical consulting. These firms handle branding, messaging, advertising, content generation, and graphic design, providing fund managers with a cohesive, professional set of collateral. They can ensure that the foundation they lay will lead to an effective marketing campaign.

Attracting Investors, Winning Allocations

It's hard to stress sufficiently the importance of marketing materials in today's alternative investment marketplace. The competition is fierce and investors are demanding. If you are going to attract investors and win allocations, you must have professional marketing materials. It's that simple. To produce quality materials that are compelling, you must make a commitment of time and money, and then hire the right firm. Just as investors look to you to achieve their investment goals, you must look to alternative marketing professionals to achieve your marketing objectives.

ANN TRAUTENBERG *is President and CEO of Boston Consulting Partners. Prior to founding BCP, Ann was Director of New Business North American Sales at Forrester Research. During her 11-year tenure, Ann helped grow the company from $1 million to $250 million in revenue. Through the IPO and multiple acquisitions, Ann and her team specialized in matching clients with top-tier analysts who provided custom*

strategic and tactical marketing as well as sales and technology guidance. Forrester worked with thousands of companies, providing feedback and insight for more effective market positioning, messaging, and differentiation strategies, which helped these companies attract, win, and retain clients. In addition, Forrester advised clients through all aspects of growth strategies, evaluation of potential acquisitions, new product development, due diligence, exit strategies, and preparation for road shows, as well as designing and implementing effective marketing programs.

Identifying and Engaging with Potential Investors

CHAPTER 3

Launching Your Fundraising Campaign

Dennis Ford

As CEO of Brighton House Associates, I have had the opportunity to call on fund managers across the globe, from New York City to Hong Kong. What I've noted after countless meetings is a wide discrepancy in marketing skills. There are the consummate marketers, and then there are those who struggle time and time again to raise capital.

In talking to managers, I have come to realize that there is a gigantic need for some rudimentary knowledge of marketing. Most have either never done outbound marketing, or they are more than a bit rusty. Before the financial crisis, it took little effort to raise funds. Today, it is much tougher, which is what gave me the idea for this book.

I realized that fund managers needed not only a marketing book that delved into the skills they must learn or brush up on but also a book that is specific to the alternative investment industry. In addition, I thought it would be helpful to take some of the outbound marketing lessons my firm has learned and share them with what I hope is an eager audience.

Previously, I wrote a book called The Peddler's Prerogative, *which explained my sales philosophy to folks interested in learning how to sell. I wrote that book because I found that most sales books focus on selling methodologies and techniques and rarely touch on how to think about the three most important aspects of sales: you, your company, and your product. Techniques are important, but so is your view of the world. So as I did there, in this chapter I include some of the philosophy behind finding investors.*

Finding investors is kind of like fishing. Number one: they are either there or they're not. Number two: if they are there, you need to know how to catch them. To catch a fish you have to think like a fish, no matter how weird it gets (my friend Demi buys Storm Lures with that saying on the package). The same concept applies to finding new investors.

If there aren't any investors around, then there are none to be had. I know that is stating the obvious, and it probably seems ridiculous to point out, but many managers spend a lot of time looking for potential investors in the wrong places and are shocked when they come up with nada.

So where do you find prospective investors? Before I discuss where, let's talk about how.

I have a healthy disregard for the players in the industry who do not understand that marketing is a profession and that marketing funds is a full-time job. Many managers think fund marketing is a no-brainer, something they can do themselves in their spare time.

If that's you, think again. Raising capital in today's economic environment is highly competitive. It takes professionalism, experience, and a constant and focused effort. Marketing is an expertise that takes years to learn and perfect. Without someone dedicated to creating and executing marketing campaigns, and keeping a steady hand on the tiller, you won't achieve your fundraising goals.

So your first step should be to designate a chief marketer. Maybe it's your partner or someone from your marketing or investor relations staff. Maybe you have to hire one. Or, maybe it's you. Welcome to my world.

Marketing alternative investments is unlike marketing almost anything else. Even if you've been in the industry, times have changed. Marketers today have to wrap their minds around the new normal.

OK, back to the question of where you find potential investors. A potential investor can surface in any number of ways. You might find a firm on the Web, see a name in a database, get a tip from a friend, or meet someone at a networking event. All are fair game.

Before I tell you how I find prospects for my business, let me say that prospect lists are relatively easy to come by. The hardest part for most marketers is IDENTIFYING those that are a potential fit.

Identifying Potential Investors

As a marketer, your job is to identify investor prospects as a potentially good fit or a bad fit, and then move them on or off your plate as fast as is humanly possible.

Most marketers do just the opposite. They collect prospects, hoard them even, and keep adding to their stash. They like nothing better than having a lot of potential investors. Being the optimists that they are, there's a comfort knowing there are all those possibilities in the queue just waiting for them.

If that's you, consider yourself forewarned. When marketers let themselves be seduced by long lists of prospects, they have slipped into what I call the *Marketer's Magical Reality*. They believe everything will be all right as long as they have prospect lists; lists will somehow, some way, turn into allocations. Their natural optimism is running wild, leading them into the fantastic, and heading straight toward the magical.

Listen up! You don't just want prospects, you want GOOD prospects. A few good potential investors are better than a full pipeline of poor ones. In fact, I firmly believe that it's as worthwhile spending time getting bad prospects off your plate as it is getting good ones on your plate.

Let's face it. In our fast-paced marketer world we don't have a lot of time every day to review our prospects and decide which ones we're going to pursue. We can't be indecisive or confused as to where to focus our efforts. We have to be able to grab a few and start dialing. You can do this only if you've got all good prospects.

Another reason for clearing your plate is that having a lot of prospects that are not a potential fit for your firm can obscure the ones that are.

So when you get a prospect, the first thing you must do is IDEN-TIFY it. This takes practice, discipline, and a certain amount of vigilance—but it's what successful marketers do.

But again, you don't have all day, which brings us to the concept of right investors, wrong investors, and investor profiles.

Right investors are what it's all about. If you know who a right investor is, you'll be able to separate the good prospects from the bad ones. Quick! If you're marketing an emerging fund that has assets of $20 million, should you focus your efforts on large government pension funds?

Successful firms develop a profile of their ideal investor. They analyze their funds, target market, existing clients, and so on, and create a description of the model investor. If your firm doesn't have one, create one. And if it does, verify it.

Let's say you are marketing a hedge fund that has $500 million under management. Your strategy is long/short equity, and the fund has delivered a decent performance over the past five years with the exception of 2008. The first thing to do is look at the types of investors—for example, endowments, family offices, and wealth advisors—that have invested in the past. Then find more like them.

Second, try to discover new types of investors that it makes sense to pursue. Many fund managers use investor research and data providers to identify new investor categories and find new investors. My company, Brighton House Associates, interviews investors and sells subscriptions to the mandate data we uncover through our one-on-one interviews.

Whatever you do, keep investor profiles simple and logical. That way, you'll be able to keep them in the front of your brain and quickly zero in on the good targets.

The Measurers and Analytics

Some fund managers think that the solution to the fundraising dilemma is to keep close tabs on a small group of targeted investors. Unfortunately, these managers often have no real-world marketing experience. They don't understand how finding investors works. As a result, they can turn a normal meeting about fundraising into a circus that is hazardous to the marketer's health. Fundraising is a numbers game. The more investors you call, the more prospects you'll have.

The key to keeping a harmonious office is to agree on how to categorize prospects, because ultimately, it's a conversation between you and the managing partner: "It is exceedingly difficult to appease your desire to count that investor prospect in this month's inflows, as I spoke with him for the first time only three hours ago. However, for your purposes, I can say that I've *identified* him as a prospect."

You can see where I'm heading here. You don't want to classify just any old prospect as *identified*, only a good one. Because you can be sure that next week, or next month—at some point—the managing partner will be angling to move your identified prospects onto the qualified list, and then, BLAM!, there they are on the inflow forecast. If you try to pass off bad investor prospects as good ones, you'll be doing a lot of backpedaling down the pike.

So treat every prospect as suspect. Focus on who really invests in your funds and the reasons why. Ask the tough questions. Does a prospect really fit the investor profile? Prove to yourself that a prospect is worth your time. This will help you avoid getting stuck in the *Marketer's Magical Reality*. Be ruthless. There are no maybes here. It's either yes or no. Here's a tip: if it isn't a good prospect, it's a bad one.

Grokking Your Company

After I join a company, the first thing I do is find out what the heck I'm marketing and to whom. I start walking around with my eyes and mouth wide open in earnest curiosity asking tons of questions of anyone who will listen. Depending on their answers, I'll leave pretty quickly or stay until I am thrown out. What usually happens is that I find one or two folks who I like, are smart, and I can hammer constantly. I make them my friends and then bother them all the time. What are friends for?

I ask questions and I listen and I ask more questions and I listen some more. I figure that in my first couple of fly-bys, I hit most of the obvious questions.

You need to take the same approach. The questions you need to ask, in no particular order, are:

- Who are our biggest investors?
- Why do they invest in our funds?
- Who else is similar that we have not approached yet?
- Who is the investor we can't get no matter how hard we try?
- Who in the firm is the best at marketing our stuff?
- Who really knows the fund the best?
- Who is the best investor relations person?
- What do investors like most about our funds?
- What do investors like least?
- Who is the best executive in front of investors?
- Who likes to help?
- Who doesn't like to help, but when forced is very good?

And the last question you should always put to whoever you're chatting with is this: "So, if you were me, how would you market our fund and who would you go after?"

You will get some of your best targets from asking this *simple* question constantly.

In the finding phase, the inside folks are your best resource. They can help you find potential investors and grok the fund. Then when you have one of those targets on the line and need help reeling them in, guess who you're going to call and who's going to be more than glad to help?

Fund managers may be great traders but their marketing skill sets are all over the board. In addition, some may not respect the work required to get investors in the door. So trying to convince them that you have a great prospect that's worth their time and attention can be difficult—unless, of course, the prospect you're bringing in is one they recommended.

I also find out the history of the company and the product. For these questions, you'll want to hit the executives first, then the analysts. If it's an established fund, these folks have been around for a while and know where all the bodies are buried. (Just kidding!) Founders have usually chronicled the entire goings on of the company in their heads and have been eyewitnesses to most of the pivotal moments. If you're at an emerging fund, usually there's still some history. Is it a spin-off? Who are the folks that worked together in the past? Get the lowdown.

Back to Ground Zero

After I learn the history of my company and the product, how the product works, and who's who in the zoo, I typically try to validate my obvious hunches about how I would market the product. To do this, I find the person, or persons, in-house who understand the product, all its subtleties and nuances, and is savvy about the market.

It may sound brash, but I go right back to ground zero and start validating all the assumptions and big decisions that have been made to date with regard to the product, including the positioning and marketing methodologies. I do this to make the product and the company mine.

If you are going to be a good marketer, you have to go through the magic act of taking ownership of your firm and your fund in your mind. Once they become yours in your mind, then you innately do the right things for the care and feeding of these great possessions. It's the Zen of marketing: you need to get the fund inside your head and you have to get inside the fund's head.

It usually takes me three to six months to really learn and validate a product. My goal is to know as much about the product as anyone else. Sometimes because I am fresh, I know it better than some of the in-house folks, who are stale. It is so funny when, in a relatively new position and armed with enough product knowledge to be dangerous, I go into a meeting and start spouting off. Looks of horror and surprise, mental notes all around: "Watch out for this guy." Who, me?

Don't let the three to six months fool you into thinking that in the meantime I am doing nothing, because that is far from the truth. If I don't know the product yet, I have no problem dragging the folks in the know along with me to meetings.

When you think about it, if you have to be productive from the get-go and you don't have the knowledge, it only makes sense to find someone who does. Then, while you're preparing for a meeting and traveling together, you have an expert with you for hours on end. I take full advantage of this time to get fantastic, one-on-one training. It's a fact of life: the more you know about your fund, the more money you will raise.

You can also grok the fund by spending time with the traders and other in-the-know folks. In the beginning, you may have no idea what they're all talking about. But if you hang around with them enough and listen to the ongoing dialogue, you will begin to learn the fund's strategy through osmosis. Eventually, you'll reach the point where you have a pretty thorough understanding of the fund.

In the beginning months, I also sit through countless presentations and pitches until I have them memorized along with the answers to the 25 or 30 questions that are most commonly asked. Pretty soon I can parrot the company's pitch. Having repeated this process many times over the years, I am a pretty quick study. But please make no mistake: this is a quick and dirty solution only. You need to really learn your fund and its strategy!

The Rub

Let's see, where are we? OK, you start learning about the fund, which can take as long as six months. The rub is you never have that luxury. While you're learning, you also have to find some prospects, map the organization, line up some meetings, make presentations, and get something cooking. This is the marketer's life. Deal with it.

Another funny thing about being a marketer is that the conditions under which you are marketing are almost never good. You have a new fund, which means no track record. You have a fund with a track record, but it has some performance issues. Your fund has performed well, but it requires lock-ups when liquid funds are in demand. And on and on it goes.

In marketing, everything is in more or less of a whacked-out state constantly. Your job is to keep your head screwed on straight enough to find investors despite it all.

Here's a tip that can make your job easier: market quality funds that provide a return on investment. Marketing poor performing funds to folks who don't really need them is ridiculous.

The Look-Alikes

Let's face it, whether you have a new job, a new fund, or a new territory, you don't have a lot of time to show some results. So you have to be adroit. Find the obvious prospects first, pick the low-hanging fruit, and get something cooking. Then figure out a way to get on up the tree. For example, if you are marketing to family offices, smaller pension funds and endowments tend to look just like them: they all have small teams that evaluate funds and make recommendations fairly quickly. In addition, the decision maker usually is easy to contact.

Front and Center

I keep track of my prospects on a whiteboard. It's not high-tech, but it works for me. I hang it on my wall so I have all my prospects in front of me at all times. I can always see what I have and, more important, what I don't have in the pipeline.

I suggest you do the same. Divvy up the board into three columns and assign your prospects to the appropriate category:

- *Identified.* Classify as identified investor prospects whom you have not spoken with, but who you suspect may take an interest in your fund. Maybe they have invested in funds of a similar size or with a similar strategy in the past. In short, they fit your fund's investor profile.
- *In Play.* Prospects are in play if you have contacted them and introduced your firm, they have expressed an interest, and you are beginning or maintaining a dialogue with them.
- *In Process.* Prospects are in process if you're on their short list—the investors have indicated you are one of a few select firms on which they are conducting due diligence. They are asking for more information and monitoring your performance, and you are building a relationship.

Seeing where particular prospects fall can help you decide where to spend your time. If you need to raise some capital fast and few prospects have reached the in-process stage, you might focus on a look-alike. However, if you hear that family offices are open to strategies such as yours, then maybe that's where you should spend your time.

Desperation

Trying to find potential investors can drive marketers to distraction. Perhaps you are a new marketer or new at a firm and your pipeline is empty, your inflow goal has been increased (it's never decreased), or you are facing some newfangled pressure tactic that management has contrived to get you to raise more capital. In spite of it all, on some predetermined schedule, usually monthly or quarterly, you must show your stuff and bring home the bacon.

At times like these it is very easy to fall down the desperation rat hole. You are constantly being monitored and measured. You're stressed. You allow demons inside your head. Then nothing is the same. I've seen desperate marketers walking around with a glazed look in their eyes, chanting, "Must find allocations. Must find allocations." I've seen the nicest marketers become bullies, and salt-of-the-earth marketers become delusional and psychotic. When marketers get into this state, it is not a good thing for them or anyone in their orbit.

So let's get down to the real issues that surface when a marketer is desperate. First, you lose your sense of right and wrong, and your sense of reality gets pretty fuzzy. When you are not thinking straight, you are not acting straight either. Desperate marketers do desperate things.

Second, because you have a distorted view of reality, you may lose the clarity you need to keep all your marketing stuff simple and straightforward.

Third, how can you accomplish anything when you are losing it? In short, when you let yourself become desperate, you've just given the proverbial snowball a big push down the "I'm going to run myself over" mountain.

The marketer's world is stressful and can seem desperate, especially in the finding stage, because guess what? You're always starting with nada. A marketer literally has to create something from nothing all the time. This is not for the weak of heart. It all boils down to the fact that finding opportunities is really hard, tedious work.

Keep in mind that the better you are at finding, the better you will be at marketing and securing allocations. You have to learn how to find good prospects. Don't think that once you get past the finding stage, you'll be fine. Not so. You must master this part.

Here's the key to being a good finder: knowing your firm well, having an intimate understanding of your fund, and last, but not least, having a clear understanding of the types of institutions investing in your fund.

When you feel yourself slipping into the desperate realm, pull yourself back out. Enlist the help of others if necessary. Often, marketers try to hide—or worse, deny—the problem. Don't!

The moral of the story: be honest with yourself and your managing partner. This isn't a marketer's self-help book, but if any work group needs to be hyperaware of stress and desperation it's marketers. Don't ignore it. Don't give in to it. Be on the lookout for it. Because it can kill you.

On that cheery note, it's time to take a look at more finding techniques.

Finding 102

After you've ramped up and are feeling more comfortable with your firm, the fund, and your territory, you should try other techniques for finding potential investors.

The Perfect Fit—It Just Feels Soooo Right!

Understanding the similarities between your fund and your competitors' is essential when looking for prospects. Equally important, however, is how they are different, because you can turn differences into an edge and attract investors that fit your firm's unique target profile.

Here's a tactic that's simple, yet works. Always be questioning your fund's positioning. If you do, you may find an edge that everyone's missed or glossed over. It may be insignificantly small or glaringly large. Ya, glaringly large. But the only way to find it is to constantly rethink the fund positioning. You don't need to dwell on it for hours on end; just keep it in the front of your brain and be on the lookout for something that will give you an advantage.

I don't want to cause a riot in the alternative investment world (well, maybe a little one), but I have to tell you, QUESTION, QUESTION, QUESTION everything coming out of the management team regarding how to position and market your fund. Of course they have great insight and experience, but times change and funds need to be updated and repositioned. The most relevant data in the world is what you learn in the field, first hand, from your investor prospects and your stable of current investors. The fact that this information is disregarded or misunderstood by management is a problem for marketers.

When you come up with something that might give you an edge, try it! I'm not saying to do this every time with every call. But don't stick to the script if you have something worth trying. Don't tell yourself that it's too far out or it just won't work. You won't know until you try it.

The net-net is, differences give you an edge, so find them and make the most of them.

The Marketer's Prospect Mall

I like to think of my region like a big mall—the marketer's prospect mall. Everything's conveniently in one place and I'm shopping for all kinds of deals. As at any mall, I'm interested in finding out which companies are the anchors; they are typically the marquee names. I do this for three reasons. First, I always want to know the prize accounts in my turf. Second, often there are secondary accounts that are nearby. Third, in some cases, between two anchor accounts is a corridor of companies. So locate the big names, and you're bound to find some smaller targets nearby.

This strategy pays off when you get on the road. I like to set up as many calls as I can when I'm out. If I know where the prospects are, I can line up meetings in geographical order and jam my schedule. This takes some planning, but it's important to spend most of your time in front of prospects and not driving around. When you're in an area, you might as well do as much shopping as you can, which means if your schedule isn't packed or something falls out, cold call for "that day" visits.

When you're on the road, you should end every meeting with another one of my must-ask questions: "Now that you know all about our fund, who else would you go after in this region?"

Ask this simple question to all the right people and it's amazing how much intelligence you will gather. A right person would be someone who is breathing and speaks your language.

Be the Best in Your Company

Finding deals for me is easy. I am a creative thinker, and I have a burning desire to show everyone just how gosh darn smart I am.

It is important to remember that your marketer attitude has a lot to do with your success. Before you call on an investor, you need to believe there is a fit. Then, you need to visualize yourself pitching that investor. If you've done your homework—you know your fund and your prospect—and you're not skirting the *Marketer's Magical Reality*, then you can go in with confidence.

Also keep in mind that tenacity is key when raising capital. You may get unequivocal noes the first several times you call on a new investor. If you persevere, however, you will get a meeting eventually. I like it when I get a no, because then I have to figure out how to get a yes. I look at it this way: any company I think is a right account will eventually be a customer of mine. They just haven't realized it yet!

Of course, sometimes everything's right but the timing. If you see a fit but you're too early, be patient, wait for the right moment, and then strike! At Brighton House, we've tracked our hit rate over a 3-year period, and we've learned that it takes as many as 10 to 15 calls to get 1 callback. And that callback often is only to tell us who we should be speaking with. Then it's another 10 to 15 calls to reach that person. To chat with the "right person" once a quarter usually requires 5 to 7 calls. We have calculated that it takes 90 minutes per year to keep a single investor's mandate information current.

Keep It Real

Look at marketing from the perspective of the folks at the other end of the phone or on the other side of the desk. They probably get tons of calls every day from bothersome, pushy fund marketers. So your first goal is to bring some humanness to the conversation.

This may seem like I'm emphasizing the obvious, but being a good marketer is all about simple concepts and truths. When you bring another person into your reality, then you have a place in theirs. When you become a real live person to another person, he or she holds a place for you inside themselves, and that spot gets reactivated when you call again. Eventually, the person you keep calling will get to know you, and when that happens, a relationship begins.

I have this crazy notion that giving people a glimpse of my life at any particular moment is amusing to us both. So I tend to be a color commentator on my life to just about anyone and everyone. If someone listens, then I try to engage him or her in a conversation, usually something funny, topical, or philosophical. And I use my Boston accent to the maximum when traveling outside New England. The deal is you have to try to find some common ground that takes you from being just a marketer doing your obligatory spiel to somebody who is real. Getting to be "somebody" is probably the single hardest part of the cold-calling process.

The Marketer's Truth

Before I stop yakking about finding investors, I'll leave you with some truths that I have learned along the way. First and foremost, you must get yourself into the finding mode. It's hard to go traipsing about, looking under every rock for new investors to call on. But you have to do it, and it is so much easier when you have your head into it and are fully engaged.

Don't try to go it alone. That's a waste of time. You need to ask everyone and his brother if they were you who would they go after, and then cherry pick the best suggestions. Start with the founder and managing partner, and ask which investors in your territory they would most love to have as a client. Then set up the meeting.

Successful fundraising is about getting up and away from your desk, and asking anyone and everyone who you should go after. Sure you need to come up with a bunch of investor targets on your own, but getting as much input as you can is what it's all about. Don't try to be a one-man band. Assembling your team and getting many folks engaged on your behalf is a beauteous thing.

Think out of the box. Get way out in the margins and open up your mind. The best way to find allocations is to really, really think about who would be a great prospect to call upon. Thinking is more important than action in marketing. It is imperative to create activity, but mindless activity is fruitless.

When you are thinking about how to find investors, always go to the blatantly obvious first, then to the polling method, on to the grand castle in the sky scenario, ending with the bold stroke vision. Never say never, and don't presuppose that you know anything about anything until you have picked up the phone and heard a prospect say "no way" or get laughed at in an unfunny manner.

When you get a hot prospect, stay cool and keep it under wraps. This is imperative. Marketers have a penchant for making mountains out of molehills and announcing a prospect as if they've just received an allocation. Filter yourself. Don't brag. Don't overhype your investor pipeline.

The strategies above should serve you quite handily. Onto creating a target list!

DENNIS FORD is President and CEO of Brighton House Associates and responsible for the overall business growth of BHA. He has 25 years' experience working primarily with emerging technology companies across multiple industry sectors. Dennis is an expert at using database services to create business solutions and using the Internet to create an

interactive dialog between buyers and sellers. He is a big proponent of using profiling and matching technology to find that all-important "business fit" in the marketing and selling process. He is also an expert in social networking strategies and technology. Dennis is the author of The Peddler's Prerogative, *a well-received book on selling (www.the peddlersprerogative.com).*

Prior to joining BHA, Dennis was founder and CEO of Next Phase Business Development, which invested and participated in technology companies, helping them determine the straightest line between technology and revenue. In 1998, Dennis was Vice President of Business Development at Engage Software (a wholly owned subsidiary of CMGI), where he ran the Software and Data Services Division and ramped it up to $50 million in 24 months. Dennis sits on the board of the University of Massachusetts Entrepreneurial Center, a venture start-up incubator, which brings together venture capital firms, UMass students, and start-up companies to launch new businesses.

CHAPTER 4

Researching the Investor Universe to Identify Prospects

Michael Calore

Two and a half years ago, I began cold calling for Brighton House Associates. I was given a list of firms, and I was to find each company's phone number and the appropriate contact, and then connect with that person. It seemed straightforward, so I jumped in.

I found it usually took me ten to fifteen calls to connect with someone. And my hit rate was low—1 to 2 percent of the companies on my list turned into prospects. But I believed it was strictly a numbers game—the more calls I made, the more prospects I'd get—so I persevered. Every morning, I started at the top of my list and worked my way down during the course of the day.

I did this for about six months. Then I began to think there had to be a better way. More out of curiosity than anything else, I began Googling and researching the firms before calling them. Then I began Googling and researching the person I hoped to contact. I found that a little background information went a long way on a call, so I dug deeper.

I researched the target firms' competition, searched for contacts on LinkedIn, and created a profile form where I tracked all the information I found. Not only did my calls with targets become more productive, but when I left voice mail, I was able to leave messages that resonated. The day someone called me back, I knew I was on to something.

As I researched names on my list, I also found new names to add and I became more creative in my sleuthing. For example, one day I came upon the name of a person at a family office. I had an e-mail address and the firm name, but I had no phone number and no address. There was no website. Where should I start?

I decided to look up the domain name. Sure enough, I came across a domain registration form, which had the firm's address. I Googled the address and found the building directory online. What luck! I looked through the list of companies. Nothing. The name of the family office wasn't listed. But the name of another company rang a bell. I checked it out and my hunch was right—it was the name of the company that was sold, the event that spawned the creation of the family office. I noted the number of the company and made the call. My contact's first words were, "How did you ever find me?" We had a great conversation and the office became a prospect.

The moral of the story is simple. Cold calling is a numbers game, but researching targets improves your odds. The research can be time consuming and tedious, but it also can be creative. And it certainly is more rewarding. Not only has my hit rate improved to 5 to 10 percent, but I also enjoy cold calling a lot more.

A $50 million hedge fund is looking to aggregate assets, so it spends weeks calling university endowments and U.S. government pension plans. An established $750 million hedge fund wants to expand its long-term investor base and grow its fund to $2 billion, so it diligently pursues funds of funds. Both are actively marketing their funds—and frustrated because they are getting nowhere.

Identifying the most relevant investors for your fund is the single most important aspect of fundraising. Yet many managers don't take the time to do so. Like the funds above, managers often buy a list and start dialing, without considering that government pension plans won't evaluate a small hedge fund, funds of funds aren't a source of stable and reliable capital, and numerous other nuances about the alternative marketplace. So they spend a lot of time, money, and energy contacting the wrong investors.

There is nothing more instrumental to a successful marketing campaign than a good list. A good list is one that has the types of investors who are a fit for your fund. To know who your potential investors are, however, you have to know who you are—who you are now, and who you want to be in the future.

If you are a fairly new fund that is seeking allocations of $1 million to $5 million and beginning to build up your business, funds of funds and family offices are good places to start. These investors are more apt to invest with emerging managers, and typically make smaller allocations.

If you are an established $1 billion fund that has a long track record, larger institutional investors such as pensions and endowments are your best bet. These investors usually seek funds that are reputable and have an extensive infrastructure. Also, they make much larger allocations, typically $15 million to $50 million. Because they often do not want their investment to represent more than 5 percent or 10 percent of a fund's portfolio, they seek managers with significant assets under management.

If you are a mid-sized fund looking to grow, the playing field is even larger. Most types of investors will consider a fund your size. That's the good news. The bad news is that narrowing the field to find your best targets takes a bit of work.

Countless alternative investment managers waste time and resources trying to get in front of the major players. These include endowments such as Yale, Harvard, and the University of Chicago; pensions such as New York State, CalPERS, and CalSTERS; and notable private wealth management firms. However, because of their size and requirements, they are not realistic prospects for many funds. In addition, everyone is trying to get in front of these investors, and frankly, they have hundreds of funds already in their pipelines. The odds of getting an audience with these investors are not in your favor.

A better strategy is to determine the investor categories that are right for you. Then pursue the smaller or lesser-known investors in that category who are not in the spotlight, but who actively allocate. Research the boutique family office in Cleveland that dedicates $75 million of its $500 million portfolio to hedge funds, or the $150 million fund of funds in Minneapolis that annually adds two or three funds to its portfolio. They are not receiving as many calls and may be excellent prospects.

Sourcing Potential Investors

So how do you find the investors that are right for you? If you consider the thousands of databases that claim to have the most relevant and timely data on active investors around the globe, there are countless ways to source potential investors. However, your own contact list that you've developed through networking events, conferences, and lists traded with peers is usually a better source. The best list, of course, is one that is handcrafted.

It is often worthwhile to build a list of firms that are not on everyone's radar screens. Usually, there is a reason why these investors are not well known. Sometimes it's because they want it that way. Other times, the firms are relatively new. If firms are purposely private or so new that they don't have a website or listed address, how can you find them?

The most impressive sources for identifying new targets, or targets that are less well known, are social and professional networking sites such as LinkedIn. These sites are almost unmatched by any other source, mainly because the investor profiles are actively updated and managed by the investors themselves.

The financial crisis drastically changed the investment community. Firms have closed, teams have been spun off, and people have moved from company to company. It is nearly impossible to keep up with the shifts in the alternative investment space. The beauty of social and professional networking sites is that as investors change firms or join new teams, they update their profiles. Obviously this process is completely arbitrary, and its timeliness depends on how diligently individuals update their status. Nonetheless, they are still some of the finest sources available.

Let's take LinkedIn as an example. There are many ways you can search for prospective targets on LinkedIn. I generally start broadly and gradually narrow my search. I begin by typing in keywords such as "family office," "hedge fund analyst," or even "manager selection." That instructs LinkedIn to search through all the profiles in its database and look for those keywords. Sometimes I add an industry search, which allows me to pick specific industries such as "investment management," "financial services," or "investment banking." You'll find LinkedIn does half the work for you, in that it orders the list of people by how relevant their background is to your specifications. Some low-hanging fruit is typically within the first few pages, with more challenging targets following.

Sometimes you are lucky enough to find all the information you need in an individual's LinkedIn profile: the firm's name, website, phone number—even some background on the firm, and how actively it invests in the alternative space. Other times, all you learn is that the individual is an investment analyst for XYZ Family Office in New York. Don't get discouraged, get creative.

I exhaust every outlet before walking away from a potential target. For example, recently I found the perfect target on LinkedIn. He was the CIO of a Philadelphia-based single-family office with $700 million under management. In his profile he went so far as to disclose the name of the firm and that he was in charge of fund manager due diligence for the investment portfolio. The problem? No website, no phone number, and no other employees listed.

So I typed the name of the firm into Google. Nothing. Now what? Well, I had his name, so I did a Google search on him. All that came up was his LinkedIn profile. I spent the next hour trying to find his phone number and got nowhere. Then it came to me: I know the name of the firm and I know it's based in the Philadelphia area; let me try 411. I went to 411.com, typed in the name of the firm and the region and *Presto!* I got an address and a phone number.

Persistence is the key to building a target list. I rarely give up, and if I do, it's only temporary. If I feel like I've exhausted all possible avenues, I'll give it a rest and look for another target. But I never abandon my search for long. A few weeks later, I'm back on the case—and this time I'm usually successful. All it takes is a little creativity and determination and you can compile an excellent list of potential investors. This is the most critical step in effective and efficient fundraising. It is worth the time and effort.

Drilling Down

After you have aggregated a large list of potential targets through a handful of sources, the next step is to find more information. It is important to understand who each target is in order to prioritize your efforts. It's also important to understand the MO of each investor before picking up the phone. Knowing the backstory of each target will help streamline the conversation.

So first things first: What type of investor is the target? Is it a family office, registered investment advisor, consultant, pension fund, foundation, endowment, fund of funds, or some other category? Knowing who they are will help you to plan your attack.

Next, determine if the firm is well known or a diamond in the rough. If you're trying to get in front of a multibillion-dollar multifamily office with hundreds of clients, there are probably a dozen or so people who would be good targets. However, if you have identified a small, private investment firm that has four or five employees, there is only one, maybe two, associates in charge of fund selection.

Now, do your targets invest in hedge funds? If it's a family office, especially a fairly large one, odds are it allocates a significant portion of its portfolio to hedge funds. If it's a $500 million pension with only 2 percent of its total assets dedicated to hedge fund investments, odds are it only invests in one or two hedge funds at a time.

After you have determined the type of investor, the appropriate contact, and if he or she invests in hedge funds, find out the allocation cycle. Each institution has its own allocation cycles. For instance, funds of funds are always evaluating and monitoring hedge funds for potential consideration, regardless of whether or not they are actively allocating. Pension funds and endowments, on the other hand, generally set an allocation timeline every year, which they follow until the mandate is satisfied. Family offices typically maintain a significant cash reserve and can allocate under short notice. What is the allocation cycle for your prospect?

Finally, understanding the role of the person you have identified at the target is also very important. The people you want to talk with have titles such as senior investment analyst, director of alternative investments, portfolio manager, analyst of absolute return strategies, CAIA, or CFA. These folks, especially when associated with institutional or accredited investors, typically are a good place to start. It is paramount when trying to execute an effective marketing campaign that you dedicate your time and resources trying to connect with the right individual. There is nothing worse than spending four months trying to reach someone only to find out that he or she is not the person you need to talk to.

Get Personal

Now that you have identified the firms you are going to target, as well as the individuals, it is time to learn more about each person before dialing the number. Understanding each person's background and path to the present position is important. In the alternative investment community, everyone knows everyone, or at least knows somebody who knows someone. Doing a little bit of research on your target could dramatically increase your chances of reaching him or her. For example, one of your current investors may have gone to school with one of your targets or your managing director may have worked with him or her at another firm. Connections such as these can get you in the door and give you an edge. So it's worth the time and effort to conduct some due diligence on each and every target you have in your sights.

It is also important to determine the length of time a target has worked at the current firm. LinkedIn tracks the amount of time each individual has worked in the most recent position. If I have two contacts at a target firm, sometimes I go after the person who has been there less time, especially if he or she has been there a year or less. These individuals tend to be more willing to take a call and more open to receiving information, chiefly because they are new to the firm and want to show their value. Of course, if a more senior associate is a better target in terms of position and job duties, I will pursue that person. Sometimes more senior folks are able to say more definitively if they're interested or not.

Understanding the pedigree of a firm can also play a key role in identifying good prospects. For example, if the patriarch of a family office made his fortune in oil and gas, chances are the firm probably invests in funds that are linked to natural resources. Doing the extra leg work and researching the target will set you up for a more relevant and comprehensive conversation.

Making the Calls

Now it's time to prioritize your targets and start reaching out. You can organize your list by your knowledge of investors or past relationships. You can also do it by investor category, size, or location. In most cases, the latter makes the most sense. Depending upon the extent of the investor's due diligence, the greater the distance, the more expensive it will be to secure an allocation. Some investors think the same way. If you are a $150 million hedge fund based in Greenwich, Connecticut, for example, the odds of making some serious headway with a registered investment advisor in Saudi Arabia are slim to none. A better place to start would be with the $550 million multifamily office based in Chicago; it's close enough to Connecticut and easy to get to.

The next course of action is to build a solid, cohesive, and direct approach for your pitch—one for contacting investors by phone and one for e-mail. Anticipate that you have 30 seconds to convey your message, pique their interest, and keep them listening. These folks are busy, and they don't have time for a pitch full of stutters and pauses. Keep it simple, keep it tight, and keep it concise.

When you have your pitch down, decide if you should call or e-mail. I will let the other authors go into the details of contacting investors by phone and e-mail, but I will say this: I prefer making a phone call over sending an e-mail. You can convey an enthusiasm and a personal touch when speaking with someone by phone that is hard to do in an e-mail.

When you contact potential investors, it's important to be diligent, but not annoying. I call it being professionally persistent. I have found that even when prospects are a perfect fit and are truly interested, more often than not they have so many balls in the air that they don't have the chance to follow up regularly. Therefore, you must take control of the situation and be persistent in order to stay on their radar screen. Remember: the early bird gets the worm; the squeaky wheel gets the oil.

There are many intricate aspects to orchestrating a successful marketing campaign, and fundraising, when done incorrectly, can seem a most grueling task. But if you take the time beforehand to identify and understand the most relevant investors for your fund, you will greatly increase your chances of raising capital.

MICHAEL CALORE is a Research Manager at BHA. He is responsible for developing strategic initiatives in order to continually expand the firm's coverage across the alternative investor universe. Michael also assists in the training and development of interns and new employees, and is Lead Marketer for the BHA Quarterly Research Report. Michael received a Bachelor of Science degree in Finance from Providence College.

CHAPTER 5

The Nuances of Effective E-Mail Campaigns

Daniel McDermott

E-mail is one of the best marketing tools. Maybe even the best. I started using it to market funds more than seven years ago, and I've never looked back. It's not only inexpensive, but it lets you easily deliver messages tailored to specific target audiences.

When I began using e-mail to market funds, it was much more time consuming and labor intensive to execute a campaign than it is today. Merging contact databases often resulted in errors that had to be fixed by hand. Most software programs provided little flexibility for personalizing messages. And computer systems were slower, so I avoided embedding graphics. During the past several years, the tools for conducting e-mail campaigns have matured and today it's much easier.

Still, many managers shy away from e-mail campaigns. One reason is the rules and regulations governing managers' interactions with potential investors. To be sure, these rules are stringent and must be followed. But with the proper legal counsel, managers can reap the benefits of e-mail while staying within the boundaries.

Another reason is that many managers fear that if prospects receive a few unsolicited e-mails, they will see them as a spammer. By all means, you should avoid blindly e-mailing investors unless you've determined that they are potential fits. This will help you adhere to the rules and regulations. It's also a good marketing practice. Investors may be a fit if they have expressed interest in, or invested in, your type of fund or strategy in the past.

As part of an overall marketing campaign, e-mail is very effective. I've learned that one of the keys to successful e-mail campaigns is repetition. Many organizations use spam filters. In addition, investors are inundated with e-mail. If a message doesn't get caught by a spam filter, chances are it will get lost in the clutter and fall through the cracks. In the end, a very small percentage of unsolicited e-mail gets through.

Often, managers think that no response to an e-mail indicates that the recipient is not interested. However, even if you send out multiple e-mails, not receiving a response is not a true indicator of a prospect's interest in your fund. More than likely, for one reason or another, the recipient did not get it or did not see it.

A little-acknowledged side benefit of e-mail campaigns is that they make phone campaigns more effective. After sending a couple of messages to a list, I start making calls. After introducing myself, very often the prospect will say, "Oh, yes. I saw your e-mail." That's music to my ears. No longer am I cold calling. I now have a better chance for a successful conversation.

One of the most valuable and cost-effective tools available to a marketer of hedge funds is e-mail marketing. It allows you to introduce your firm to potential investors for a cost and on a scale unmatched by other forms of marketing.

The ease of developing and executing an e-mail marketing campaign also makes it one of the most widely used—and abused—tools in the industry. The broad usage has not only created a lot of noise but also a great deal of spam. The challenge for your fund is to create an effective e-mail campaign that stands out from the crowd and avoids the "spam" moniker.

This chapter discusses the current strategies and tools effective fund marketers use to create compelling e-mail marketing campaigns that get results, while remaining fully compliant with spam regulations.

Note, too, that when marketing a fund, you must have a clear understanding of federal and state regulations that govern marketing to potential investors. Your firm's legal counsel should provide you with their interpretation of the regulations, so you will be compliant in your fundraising efforts.

E-Mail as a Marketing Strategy

E-mail marketing is an excellent way to introduce your firm to new investors. The obvious benefit of an e-mail campaign is its breadth of coverage. It can cover a large target audience in less time than a phone canvassing effort. It is also more economical than a snail-mail campaign. Usually the factors that make marketers consider e-mail as a viable option are time and resources. No other form of marketing gets your message in front of larger pools of prospective investors in less time and for less money than e-mail.

E-mail marketing is typically used to deliver a direct message. For example, an e-mail blast is an ideal way to lay the groundwork for a road show. An initial e-mail can announce an upcoming trip, deliver all the key facts about your fund, and explain why a meeting might make sense. However, it also can be used as an icebreaker. Some investors may need to hear more before they commit to an introductory meeting. For those, e-mail campaigns open the door, making it easier for marketers to place calls and begin conversations.

The Fundamentals

Many factors come into play when creating e-mail campaigns for maximum results, so it's important to have a good understanding of the fundamentals.

In the United States, the CAN-SPAM Act is a law that spells out guidelines marketers must follow in order to avoid having their e-mail messages be legally classified as spam. According to the Federal Trade Commission, the law requires:

- E-mail headers, including the "To," "From," "Reply To," and routing information, not to be false or misleading
- Subject lines to accurately reflect the content
- Messages to tell recipients who you are and where you're located
- Messages to tell recipients how to opt out of receiving future e-mails from you
- Senders to honor opt-out requests promptly
- Marketers to monitor what others do on your behalf

When you add in the regulatory issues connected with operating an alternative investment fund, you have to be extra vigilant about doing things right. As requested throughout this book, please make sure that you have a deep understanding of the legal landscape and government regulations that are involved with the marketing of your fund.

Beyond the basic legal guidelines there are also generally accepted best practices that should be followed to ensure your e-mail campaigns avoid the spam connotation. One such practice, as discussed in Chapter 1, is having a general knowledge of the recipients and whether they are generally qualified to receive your e-mail.

Another way to ensure the legitimacy of your campaign is to screen for preexisting interest. An institution might seem a decent prospect just based on its size, location, and category. However, if you are able to determine its current search interests by, say, strategy—such as distressed, global macro, or long/short equity—then the legitimacy of your e-mail campaign will be greatly improved.

There is a benefit to screening potential recipients: a much higher hit rate. The hit rate—or the number of calls or meetings scheduled as a percentage of total e-mails sent—for a typical mass-market e-mail is 1 to 2 percent. Targeted e-mail campaigns, on the other hand, that use screening tools to predetermine a specific interest, have yielded results as high as 5 to 15 percent.

Of course, the best way to ensure legitimacy is to use a list of investors who have told the list generator, or announced publicly, that they have open mandates and are looking for managers like you.

Nearly all commercial investor-contact lists are composites of historical information on a respective limited partner, or LP. Basic contact and employee data, as well as previous investment history, may paint a picture of the investor but add little in the way of *current* interest. Obtaining current information is vital to a targeted e-mail campaign.

When Brighton House analysts interview global investors, they explain to them that their information is being recorded and will be sent along to managers who fit their search mandate. Implicit in the mandate interview is the understanding that the investor is providing specific search information in order to hear from managers who fit those criteria. Investors should never be confused as to why they received your e-mail. If it's a fit, your message will be viewed as a part of their business.

The List

Now that we understand the fundamentals of an e-mail campaign, we are ready to take the first step: creating the recipient list. The obvious questions are: Who should be on the target list, and how big should it be?

Generally, managers have an internal database of investor contacts—a list of current, past, and prospective LPs—that they have built up over the years. To augment such a list, you can purchase one of the hundreds of commercially available databases or take some time to research potential investors.

There are occasions when you will send e-mail to your entire list. Frequently, however, you will want to create sublists for particular marketing efforts. If you are targeting a single investor category, such as funds of funds, or you are planning a road trip in Europe, you should create a sublist from the master for that campaign, which brings us to the next question: How big should a list be?

Here's a good benchmark to use: for every 100 contacts, expect to schedule a conference call or meeting with one or two investors. This is a minimum level, and you are aiming for better results, but it is a good standard. Now keep that in mind and work backwards. If you're planning a marketing trip and your target list has only 150 names, expecting to fill a weeks' worth of meetings is not realistic. You should either expand the list or shorten your trip. These numbers are never exact, but they are a good place to start when planning a campaign.

After you have the data for a target list, the next step is to put the data into a manageable format. Data comes in all types of formats—particularly if you purchase lists—so it is important to get it into one you can work with. Most bulk e-mail service providers, as well as internal e-mail programs, manage data in the comma-separated values, or CSV, format, which can be manipulated and managed in Microsoft Excel.

Using Excel, separate the data into columns. Use separate columns for first name, last name, e-mail address, company name, city, state, and country. Putting the first and last names in separate columns gives you the flexibility to personalize greetings using a mail-merge option. I have always found using first names in messages delivers the best response; using first and last names seems to draw attention to your message as being a processed e-mail.

In addition to the contact information, create columns for any other pertinent data that helps to screen investors, such as current strategy interest, investor category, assets under management, and so on. For e-mail campaigns it is important to list the data by contacts, not companies, for ease of manageability.

After separating the data, sort the contacts by those with e-mail addresses and those without. Unless you plan to find the e-mail addresses for the latter group, consider deleting them, rather than having them waste space in your list.

A common mistake marketers make is using the data as is. You must make the data uniform. Some list providers capitalize names; others use upper- and lowercase. Some include courtesy titles such as Ms. or Mr. and professional titles such as Dr.; others don't. You should make sure the format is consistent and does not contain any random data, capitalizations, and so on. Also make sure to put titles in a separate column, rather than as part of the name. You don't want to find yourself sending an e-mail with the greeting: Dear Dr. Bob. Furthermore, inconsistencies can cause problems later with mail-merge options and e-mail applications.

If you've downloaded data into your spreadsheet, make sure the data match up. All it takes is one mix-up when downloading data to misalign the contact information. Eyeball your list. Does everything line up? Look for names you know. Is their contact information correct? Do the contacts' company names match their e-mail addresses? I can't tell you how many times I have sorted a list and been ready to upload it to my e-mail software only to realize that the names and e-mail addresses are off. Nothing kills the potential for an e-mail blast faster than calling recipients by the wrong name. It makes it clear that they are on the list of a firm that operates hastily.

Another common problem with commercial contact databases is the inclusion of general, rather than individual, e-mail addresses. A major selling point of investor contact databases is that they provide e-mail addresses for prospective investors. E-mail addresses are often hard to attain for the obvious reason that the owners do not want to receive unwanted solicitations. In an effort to include as many addresses as possible, many list providers include firm e-mail addresses in their list.

So if you've purchased a list, inspect it for e-mail addresses such as "info@" or "contact@." I have seen whole firms—five to ten employees—all with the same general e-mail address. Some bulk e-mail systems will treat e-mails to the same address as unique if you use a different name. That said, if you decide to use general e-mail addresses in your marketing campaigns, I recommend sending them to the person at the firm who is most involved with manager due diligence.

The next step is to review the recipients on the list. The goal here is to remove all those investors who, for whatever reason, should not be receiving your e-mail. For example, if the e-mail campaign is for a marketing road show, and you are requesting a meeting to introduce yourself and your firm, it would not be appropriate to include current LPs or firms that know you well. If you want to meet with investors and prospects you know, those meetings should be scheduled by making direct contact, either by phone or e-mail.

In addition, if you have investors who have asked to be removed from your list, you need to honor their request. Nothing creates more discord between you and your prospects than receiving repeated and unwanted solicitations following requests to be removed from your list.

As you review the names on your list, you also need to be cognizant of the relationship you have with the contacts and their firms. If an investment official from a smaller institution, such as a family office, requests to not be contacted, his decision may also cover the remainder of his team, because of the high likelihood of close collaboration. Sometimes though, the person opting out is lower on the food chain. In this case, you, as a savvy marketing professional, may decide to keep this person's boss on your list, as he or she may see your offering and decide a meeting does make sense. Coming into a firm through another channel or at a higher level sometimes is the difference between getting a meeting and getting no response.

Even if it is overkill to shoot an entire contact list if only one person opts out, the larger question remains: Who should you contact at a large firm with multiple analysts? If you don't know who researches or evaluates managers, for example, should you send e-mail to all the contacts listed?

This question falls into a gray area—an area that outbound marketing professionals in the alternatives world often find themselves in. The goal is to reach an audience that is large enough to achieve your targeted hit rate. At the same time, you don't want to dilute the impact of your e-mail by sending it to the wrong people.

The answer is: do your homework. Find the right person. This is imperative, because ultimately fund marketing is relationship-driven and you do not want to burn your firm's brand capital by appearing to be too cavalier with your effots. As a fund marketer, you must reach out to enough people to make sure that your message reaches investors who are a fit, while always being aware of the way your message is being received by your prospects.

Now that you have the final list from which you are going to launch the e-mail campaign, it's time to think about distribution.

E-Mail Marketing Software

After your list has been vetted, screened, and cleaned, it's time to select an e-mail software program to deliver your messages. There are basically two ways to send e-mail. If you have a small list, you can send e-mail to single recipients. For lists of more than 20 recipients, however, it makes sense to use the functionality of e-mail software designed for this task.

The benefits of using e-mail marketing software are many, as more and more marketing professionals have discovered. As a result, the industry—and, more to the point, the number of programs to choose from—has grown significantly.

Today, companies such as Constant Contact, iContact, and VerticalResponse offer Web-based e-mail marketing platforms that greatly reduce the time and effort it takes to produce and distribute the many e-mails associated with your marketing campaign.

The first benefit of these platforms is ease of use. Their websites provide step-by-step instructions on how to upload and manage your e-mail list, create e-mail messages, send them, and track the campaign. If you created a list in a program such as Excel, you can upload it to one of these e-mail platforms.

To create e-mail messages, many of these platforms offer tools as robust as your desktop word processor. All the applications I have sampled have the basics, including formatting and spell checking. Many offer advanced features that allow for embedded links and HTML design. In fact, the three providers mentioned earlier collectively offer more than 200 templates to help you get started. Or you can create your own using their "quick start" options, which allow you to keep the template simple, so you can skip directly to writing the body.

One of the great features of these e-mail marketing platforms is the "schedule delivery" tool. This allows you to create an e-mail message and choose the day and time it will be sent. I use this feature often. It lets me create an e-mail campaign during normal work hours in the U.S. and then schedule it to be sent to, say, London prospects at 4 a.m. There's no need for me to be up at that hour to hit the Send button. This little option allows me to prepare a campaign when the creative bug hits, schedule it, and then forget about it.

There are several other advantages to using bulk e-mail software. It is anti-spam compliant, and thus usually has much higher delivery rates than other programs. It has the capability to handle the delivery of e-mail to 500 or 1,000 recipients. And after the e-mail is sent, this software can monitor the campaign. Using tracking dashboards, you can see the percentage of recipients who opened the e-mail, clicked on the links, or requested to be removed from the list. Going a step further, e-mail marketing platforms also can list the e-mail addresses of the recipients that carried out any of these actions. Beyond this, there are often analytical tools to graph and compare recipient opens or clicks by location.

Of great value is the ability of these platforms to manage the opt-out requests of your recipients. Although the e-mails are sent through the systems' own e-mail servers, all messages appear to be coming directly from you, and all responses from the recipients are sent directly back to you. However, these systems include opt-out links and manage the responses.

The opt-out link is usually located in the footer of the e-mail. Not only is this a necessary requirement to avoid being considered spam, but it is efficient for the folks receiving your e-mail. When recipients opt out, usually these platforms let them specify the types of messages they don't want to receive. Then the platform implements their request to make sure that they are not unwittingly included in an e-mail campaign. In fact, many platforms never allow that contact back on your list, thus saving you from accidentally uploading a list with that recipient in the future.

E-Mail Campaigns

Fund marketers generally use e-mail campaigns for three main purposes:

- To set up road shows and introductory marketing trips
- To send out company announcements
- To provide prospective investors with marketing materials, including performance reports

All of these have one thing in common: they are all a way of trying to start or continue a conversation with the recipients.

E-mail campaigns to set up a road show or introductory marketing trip generally are looking to begin a conversation with potential investors, and therefore offer an introductory meeting. Keep in mind that investors receive hundreds of e-mail introductions every week. Not only should the messages be short and to the point, but attachments should be as well. A compelling one- or two-page summary of your fund is all you need.

After you schedule a meeting with an investor, and prior to your arrival, it is advisable to send a direct e-mail with some introductory information. Avoid the common mistake of overwhelming the recipient with data at this point.

After a call or meeting, follow up with the investor, sending additional information as needed or requested. Keep in mind the requisite "cooling off" periods following an introduction and the necessary rules to abide by. This is just one of the many rules and regulations set up by the SEC; make sure you are abiding by all of them. Have your marketing campaigns vetted by your law firm or compliance officer.

Announcement campaigns are a good way to stay current in investors' minds. Some announcements are operationally focused, such as a company move to larger or more prestigious offices. More than just letting your prospects know how to reach you, such e-mails can have unintended benefits, such as an institution realizing you are now in its backyard and it makes sense to get together. Other announcements may be about employees or company milestones.

The tone of announcement e-mails should be one of a discussion continued. The purpose of the e-mail is to move your relationship along; the wording and your message should convey a feeling of expectation—that you are looking forward to reconnecting.

Another common e-mail campaign is one built around marketing materials or monthly or quarterly fund reports. Investors' in-boxes are packed with this sort of correspondence, so it is important to infuse your monthly and quarterly updates with a sense of personality. Keep the e-mail body brief but engaging. Report on the most recent numbers and asset size, and perhaps allude to recent opportunities or the lack thereof. If your firm has some positive news, consider mentioning it as well. However, avoid bolding or capitalizing text. These are the tools of the desperate marketer.

Something to avoid in performance e-mails are small type and templates that display only the numbers. These can cause investors' eyes to glaze over. In addition, consider putting the important data—such as monthly performance numbers, asset size, or a recent exit multiple—in bold. This allows prospective investors to scan the e-mail and pick out the key points without having to read the entire message.

Whatever the purpose of your campaign, remember that you are one of hundreds of fund e-mails these investors are receiving every day. If you don't allow them to pick out the key points quickly, your message may never be read.

The E-Mail

Now that we have discussed the uses of e-mail marketing, let's tackle the creation of the e-mail and its two key components: the subject and the message.

The Subject

The subject is the first thing your recipients see, and it often dictates whether your message is opened and read. In fact, some studies report that 90 percent of the time the subject alone determines whether a recipient will read your message. The importance of how you phrase the subject cannot be overestimated.

In general, it is best to make the subject long enough to explain the purpose of the e-mail, but also short enough for the reader to grasp the purpose quickly—as long as it is stated in a simple and straightforward manner.

E-mail campaigns conducted to set up meetings for a road trip receive the highest open and response rates when they tell the potential investor exactly what they are seeking. Remember, investors receive hundreds of e-mails every week from managers vying for their attention. An e-mail that quickly explains the purpose of your communication and cuts through the "noise" often results in a higher open rate. So the first thing to do is begin the subject with the purpose of your message: "Meeting Request."

Next, give the investor you are contacting a little context—tell him or her who you are. One option is to use the name of the firm: "Meeting Request—Manager of XYZ Capital." Another option is to use a manager's name to make the e-mail have more of a personal touch: "Meeting Request—John Smith, Manager of XYZ Capital." You can adjust the style and format to your liking, but always be experimenting to find a subject that gets the highest response rate.

Note the use of dashes in the subject lines above. Spacing characters such as these can help potential investors quickly scan the e-mail header and decide if they want to read it. A subject heading that is easy to scan means that your e-mail will get considered. If your subject heading contains a lot of info without allowing for prospects to easily digest its meaning, they usually hit the delete button. So after stating the purpose of your e-mail, use a spacing character for ease of reading,

The next step is to complete the heading with the final details of the marketing trip, which is the location and date. An option is to keep it broad: "Meeting Request—Manager of XYZ Capital, California Trip, July 7-12." Or you could mention the cities: "Meeting Request—Manager of XYZ Capital, Trip to LA and SF Bay area, July 7–12."

In some cases, you may want to keep the location purposely broad—even if you don't have the flexibility to visit other cities. The reason is simple: the wider the area, the higher the response rate. Investors outside the target area who respond to your message can easily be converted into conference calls or meetings on another trip. The point is, you want to establish relationships with as many prospects as possible, so target as broad an area as is reasonably possible.

E-mail campaigns for marketing trips usually benefit from multiple attempts to reach prospects. It is important that subsequent attempts be reflected in the subject heading. In many cases, your original e-mail message never reached its target, was deleted before it was reviewed, or simply got lost in cyberspace. With the large amount of e-mail communication received by investors, you can assume that about half of the recipients never saw your original e-mail or didn't recognize who it was from. So it is usually best practice to attempt a second e-mail campaign to your target audience after removing those who responded to your original e-mail.

In many cases, a second e-mail attempt can have a higher response rate than the original e-mail. The primary reason for this rests in the wording of the subject. At the very start of the subject line, include the words "2nd Attempt." Follow this with the original e-mail heading. For example, "2nd Attempt—Meeting Request—Manager of XYZ Capital, California Trip, July 7-12." By making recipients aware that you have tried to reach them previously, they are more likely to review your e-mail.

Finally, as you approach the date of your marketing trip, you may have meeting slots open and prospective investors you have not heard from. A different e-mail technique can be applied here. The format of this type of e-mail usually is shorter than your original one. The purpose of the truncated format is to express a sense of informality: on the eve of the trip, you are dashing off an invitation for a last-minute meeting. The informality of the e-mail, along with the quickly approaching date, usually results in higher response rates from investors who are moved to respond, since you are going to be in their area soon.

The subject is key to using this technique effectively. Instead of the more formal "Meeting Request," it should take the form of a short note to a colleague asking for the meeting. For example, "Possible Meeting Next Week in LA?" Note that you want to be more specific with the location in this type of e-mail. You can also use this type of e-mail during the trip as well to fill in any remaining slots. Simply change "Next Week" to "This Week." The informal style and short time frame usually results in shaking a few investors free.

The Message

After constructing a compelling subject that gets prospects' attention, you need to write a message that holds their interest and results in action. The trick is to adequately explain your purpose for contacting them without making the message too long.

For our purposes here we are going to deal with general e-mail marketing campaigns and not touch on specific correspondence to LPs with whom you are already communicating.

To construct an e-mail message that results in a dialogue with a prospect, it is best to divide the message into short, concise paragraphs. Ideally, you want the body of the e-mail to display directly on the screen when your recipient opens it. At most, the recipient should have to scroll down once if he or she is using a compressed reading pane. Aim for two to four paragraphs, each comprising two to four sentences that explain who, what, when, where, and how.

The first paragraph is your introduction. It should explain why you are reaching out and offer the investor a reason to continue reading. If you want to schedule a meeting, you may want to introduce your firm, and say what you do and why you are reaching out: "I hope this e-mail finds you well. I am a partner at XYZ Capital. I will be traveling to London next week and I wanted to see if a meeting makes sense." If you have never met before, sometimes it helps to say that you don't believe the recipient has been introduced to your firm or has worked with your firm in the past.

If the e-mail is an announcement, in addition to explaining why you are reaching out also summarize the (hopefully positive) news. Again, should the recipient have a small reading pane that only displays a few sentences, you want to make sure that you are clear, concise, and compelling so he or she can get the gist and be intrigued to read further.

The few short paragraphs following the introduction should explain your purpose in a bit more detail. The ultimate goal is to get your prospect to act, so the body of the e-mail is simply a tool used to create communication. Many marketers fail in this respect. They think they need to put all their cards on the table and include a lot of details. Or they believe that investors only want the quantitative data or numbers. As a result, their communiqués are long and wordy or read like an annual audit statement, which only encourages the prospect to click the Delete button.

Remember, your prospects are human and thus the common metrics of marketing apply, regardless of their knowledge of quantitative finance. You have only a few seconds, assuming that your prospects have decided to read your e-mail, to capture their interest, convey your purpose, and get them to act. You need to be concise.

Remember, too, that e-mail campaigns make up the initial stages of your marketing efforts. Ask yourself what you are trying to accomplish. If it is to get a meeting, then create an e-mail that will get a meeting, nothing else. If it is to get an investor to inquire about your firm, then that should be your focus. There will be time down the road to detail the numbers.

Depending on your purpose, you may want to include a short paragraph about your firm or fund. Mention key metrics that will pique the reader's interest, such as asset size, track record, or performance. If the portfolio manager has been successful, mention how and where. If the announcement is about a specific event or recent performance, always mention a few details related to the data point. The goal here is to use just enough data to help your prospect understand your e-mail and to leave enough questions unanswered so there is interest in getting to know more.

The final section of your e-mail communication, and one you should always end with, regardless of the format or length, is the action section. This is the portion of your e-mail that—in a few words or a few sentences—summarizes the purpose of your e-mail and asks your prospect to act. The key here is to be specific and avoid generalities. Also remember that your reader will react based on how you phrase your conclusion.

If the purpose of the e-mail is to meet with an investor on a road trip, then conclude by asking for a meeting by giving a specific day or range of days. The easier it is for the prospect to "have to" answer yes or no, the higher your response rate is going to be. If you are sending an e-mail announcement about the firm, don't conclude by simply saying he or she can contact you with questions. That is obvious. Be specific. Say you are in the office this week and can discuss the results today or tomorrow.

Overall, if you get to the point, state it clearly, and back it up with key data points, your e-mail will have a better chance of cutting through the clutter and noise, grabbing the investors' attention, and getting them to act.

You may wonder how to craft a message to investors you have spoken with in the past, but are not actively communicating with. If it has been six months or more since you last spoke, it is probably a good idea to refresh their memory on your firm and fund strategy, highlighting growth in areas such as assets under management, firm size, or new products. Never assume that investors know or remember exactly what you do. Every day since your last meeting, your prospects have been speaking with and reviewing countless other managers. When in doubt, always err on the side of re-explaining and re-introducing your fund and putting investors in context with what your firm is doing today.

The tone of these e-mails should also be more conversational than an e-mail blast. The point is to engage your contact in a more informal manner, as if to pick up on your last conversation. To use the roadshow example, you could first begin by stating the topic of the e-mail and why you are reaching out: "I am going to be back in San Francisco next week. When we last met nine months ago, you were researching XYZ strategies. I wanted to circle back to meet and give you an update on my firm."

Before distributing an e-mail to prospects, many managers and marketers often feel compelled to include an attachment—sometimes many. There is the common misunderstanding that more is better. In addition, they assume that investors are mass consumers of fund data with a limitless appetite for even the most inane details of a fund's strategy.

For an introductory e-mail, it is usually best to limit the number of attachments to one or two. Perhaps a one- or two-page firm overview or the most recent manager commentary. Remember your goal and avoid the temptation to overwhelm them with data. E-mail campaigns are meant to whet investors' appetite, not answer every possible question they might have.

Summary

When done correctly, e-mail marketing can be one of your most effective fundraising tools. No other form of outbound communication can get your firm's message in front of such a large number of qualified investor prospects in such a short time and for such a reasonable cost.

The ultimate value of e-mail marketing, though, is highly dependent on the quality of its craftsmanship and execution. By ensuring that recipients are the right targets and qualified to receive your message, the subject is crisp and easy to grasp, and the e-mail message concisely explains your purpose and asks for action, you are creating a quality campaign.

A well-designed e-mail campaign will achieve a higher hit rate, result in more successful fundraising, and gain you respect in the alternative investment community. Your prospects will recognize that you value their time and interest, and have gone to great lengths to make sure your message arrives in a timely fashion and professional manner.

Dan McDermott is founder of Brighton House Associates and CEO of Parker Point Capital, a wholly owned subsidiary of BHA and a registered broker-dealer. As an industry veteran, Dan saw a need to market hedge funds more effectively and efficiently. He launched BHA and pioneered the concept of matching alternative investors with fund managers based on investors' mandates. This was a significant departure from the marketing approach widespread at the time, in which fund managers pursued alternative investors indiscriminately. Dan also led the development of BHA's software platform that automates the matching of investors and fund managers. Prior to founding BHA, Dan was co-founder and Managing Director of Coastal Partners, Ltd., a multidisciplinary alternative investment firm that specialized in marketing hedge fund vehicles to sophisticated clients in Europe, Asia, and the Americas.

CHAPTER 6

The Ins and Outs of Phone Canvassing

Renee Astphan and CT McLean

Fifty thousand calls. Who would have thought we could make so many? Certainly not us. When we started at Brighton House, we felt lucky to make our weekly quotas. Gradually, we learned a few tricks of the trade and began to meet our goals a little earlier each week. But still, we never would have predicted this. Calling people we didn't know was not our strong point—at least we didn't think so.

However, over the past few years we have come to realize that several things have enabled us to succeed in making so many calls. The first was researching our investor targets. Calling a firm and person whom we had researched and we believed may have a genuine interest in or need for our product was completely different from blind cold calling. Research confirmed our purpose and gave us the confidence to make calls. And when our targets realized we had considered their interests and were calling with good reason, they were more apt to be receptive, which reinforced our confidence to make the next call.

Pitching a product that had value was another critical factor. If you don't think highly of your product, it is hard to market it day in and day out. It is an unusual person who can succeed at cold calling without having enthusiasm for their product. Having a valuable product kept us dialing. Take it from us, there are days when you won't reach a single target and the world looks pretty bleak. Knowing we were marketing a product that had value helped us through those tough times.

Finally, we learned that cold calling is about meeting people, albeit by phone, having conversations, and establishing relationships. When we looked at it that way, we could lose our fear. We could relax, find some common ground, and have a worthwhile discussion—just as we would in a face-to-face meeting. And the more calls we made, the easier it got, and the more we enjoyed it. Who knew?

Gone are the days when hedge fund marketers simply had to answer the phone to speak with investors who were ready to pull the trigger on an allocation. Times have changed. Today, you must seek out potential investors, and phone canvassing is essential to the task.

Phone canvassing can be likened to martial arts. To be successful requires intense training, an in-depth understanding of your target, and discipline. It also takes a thick skin and persistence. Our statistics show that it often takes 10 to 15 phone calls just to receive one callback, and another 10 to 15 to engage in a meaningful conversation. You can't get discouraged. You must take it in stride and move forward. In a day that consists of 100 phone calls, one great conversation must be considered an achievement.

Training for the Task

Successful phone canvassing starts with proper training. Whether you're new to canvassing or just a bit rusty, it's worthwhile to take the time to learn or brush up on the skills and techniques. The resources may be at your fingertips. Are there experienced marketing executives in your firm? Shadow them and listen in on their calls. There is a wealth of information you can glean. In the beginning, listening in on calls will help you get a feel for the process, what to expect, and the pace. At the same time, you will learn about your company and fund and how best to present them to investors. Then, after a while, you'll pick up the nuances and tidbits that make good marketers great marketers.

After you've spent some time listening to the pros, ask other marketers to participate in mock phone calls. Practice answering questions and defusing a barrage of rebuttals with a calm and confident demeanor. Some investors will want to know more about your company and why they should talk with you before they give you a minute of their time. You may have to answer several questions before you ask even one. Don't let this throw you. Be prepared.

If you are the sole marketer in your firm, look to outside firms for training and support. Find ones that are familiar with the industry, as they will be able to role play as well as listen in on your calls and coach you afterwards. Such firms can help you be productive from day one.

Understand Your Targets

After you have identified your target companies and practiced extensively, you can pick up the phone and start dialing, right? Wrong. Phone canvassing also requires an understanding of the individuals you're trying to reach. Some marketers take the ready, fire, aim approach to calling investors. Don't let that be you. Before calling an investor for the first time, gather some background information. Brief yourself on the basics. What does the organization do? What types of investments have they made in the past? Who is the contact you should be speaking with?

Here's a tip: answering this last question is imperative if you want to increase your hit rate, and you can usually find this information simply by looking at the company's website or by doing a LinkedIn search. If you call the administrative assistant to find out the name of an appropriate contact, there is a very good chance you will be sent directly to voice mail rather than connected with the person, asked to leave a message, or told to send your information to the company's general address so that he or she can respond if interested. In other words, it is a good way to quickly hit a dead end, become frustrated, and lose hope early in the game. So don't underestimate this piece of advice. Before picking up the phone, make every attempt to find out who exactly you need to speak with at the company.

There are two other things you should also know before calling: your contact's title and his or her role in the fund's research process. Sometimes you can deduce a person's role from their title, but not always. So make the effort to check.

After you have identified the correct contact, the next thing to determine is when to call. It may seem obvious, but you need to be aware of time zones—which one you're in and which one your prospect is in. If you're calling Europe from the U.S. East Coast, the best time to call is in the morning up until 11 a.m. or noon. If you're in Europe and calling investors on the East Coast, try during your afternoon hours. To reach investors on the West Coast, European marketers must call during their evening hours. Marketers on the West Coast must wake up early in order to reach Europe before the end of the work day. Scandinavia is an hour or two ahead of most Western European countries, so contacts in those countries need to be called even earlier in the morning from the United States. At Brighton House, we regularly schedule some analysts to work evening hours in order to reach Asian investors and early mornings to reach those in the Middle East.

You should also be aware of lunch times and market hours. Some people disappear from their offices from 11 a.m. to 1 p.m. or from noon to 2 p.m. Others will be eating at their desk hoping for some peace and quiet, so it may be worth trying to reach an investor during lunch. Still others prefer to be contacted outside of local market hours, either early in the morning or late in the day.

Be mindful of cultural nuances as well. For example, lunch is the largest meal of the day in Spain, and people there often eat later than in other countries. It's not unusual for an investor to be on a lunch break for two to three hours in mid-afternoon. Investors in the Middle East don't work on Fridays; their work week is Sunday through Thursday. Most government pension funds in the United States are closed by 4 p.m., and in Europe, some close at 3 p.m., especially on Fridays.

Noting holidays is also important. The United Kingdom observes a few bank holidays, the United States observes several federal holidays, and Switzerland observes many religious holidays throughout the year.

London, New York, and Zurich are the top three financial centers for alternative investments and there are many holidays among them, but schedules can be found easily online.

Finally, be aware of holiday periods in Europe. August and December are the hardest months to reach investors in Europe, because many are on vacation for three to four weeks at a time.

In short, you can save yourself a lot of time and effort by having an awareness of the differences in time zones and cultures.

Get in the Zone

Successful phone canvassing requires adopting a canvassing mindset and then staying focused and committed to the process. Every job has its distractions. It is your responsibility to ignore interruptions and stay on task. If your friend in HR asks you to take a 15-minute break to get a coffee, politely ask if he or she can grab you a cup of joe. Immerse yourself in the process and then stay there, particularly if you're on a roll. When you're focused, you'll be energized, which not only produces a sense of pride in the task at hand but also results. People respond to people emitting positive energy.

When it comes to preparing for a phone canvassing campaign, put away all other tasks. You need to dedicate certain times for only making calls. If you try to make calls here and there throughout the day, in between doing twenty other things, you won't be as successful as if you block off bigger chunks of time during the week to devote to calls. It's important to do this because once you start making a few calls, you get in the zone and you can make 50 calls before you know it. And what is one of the tenets of marketing? IT'S A NUMBERS GAME.

The Pitch

Now that you have gone through the training, research, and preparation phases, it is time to pick up the phone and make the calls that may lead to the big bucks. But what do you say and, more important, how do you say it? Investors are busy people. In addition, they receive hundreds of unsolicited introductory e-mails and pitchbooks a week. So you have to make your initial contact memorable, or the conversation may very well be over right here.

The first step is to create a powerful yet succinct elevator pitch in which you state who you are, why you are calling, and your unique value proposition—how your fund blows the doors off its competitors. This initial pitch should be no more than one minute. The chief investment officer has a million other things to do; listening to a dime-a-dozen marketer blab on about minute details is not on the priority list for the day. So keep your pitch short, hit the main points, and tell the investor you will follow up with an e-mail including pertinent marketing materials.

You have your pitch. You make the call. Now be attentive. It is extremely important that you recognize the investor's demeanor within the first few seconds of the call. Does he or she seem rushed? Agitated? Cheerful? A rushed or hostile tone means you need to put your value proposition front and center. A more amiable attitude and you can use a lengthier approach. The only thing that is certain during phone canvassing is that each call will be different and require an alternate approach. It is up to you to adapt quickly.

Will you reach investors on the first try? Almost never. The sheer volume of marketers attempting to engage them in the same dialogue as you is mind numbing. As a result, you will most likely get their voice mail, and you are faced with a new dilemma—to leave a message or not. The choice is yours. However, if you have the person's direct line, it might be best not to be the fiftieth voice mail of their day, so try back another time. In other instances, a first voice mail is appropriate, but should always be cordial and introductory in nature. Don't leave a message that is longer than thirty seconds; your name, firm, contact number, and reason for calling are all that is necessary for the opportunity at a callback. Promise to follow-up with an initial e-mail if you do not hear back.

One week goes by and you haven't heard anything. Surprise, surprise. What do you do now? Lesser marketers might pack it in. They'll assume the investor doesn't like or doesn't need their fund, and they'll give up. Wrong wrong wrong. As we have noted, a successful marketer is persistent, but not pushy. You should try again, and just as before use voice mail. This voice mail should reference the first message you left as well as the follow-up e-mail that you sent.

If you find yourself leaving messages with an assistant time and time again, get creative. Many a marketer has fallen into the same black hole and realized the chances for a callback are now slim to none. What can you do? Engage the administrative assistant. Make note of his or her name when you first call. Then when you call back, try to strike up a conversation. Ask how he or she is doing, when he or she plans on taking some much-deserved vacation time—heck, even talk about the weather. By engaging this person, he or she may reveal a small but significant and helpful tidbit of information.

Some assistants won't be drawn into a conversation no matter how hard you try. In that case, reference the fact that you've left messages before and maybe it would be easier to send an introductory e-mail. Avoid falling into the trap of simply dialing a number and staying boxed in. That is doom for a marketer. Be creative. Look at other angles.

The Follow-Up

Follow-up is an integral component of the phone canvassing process. If there is one thing you need to understand about the allocation process in the alternative investment industry it's that it is lengthy and time consuming. It is not uncommon to get off the phone with an investor feeling like you just had the best conversation, she or he is extremely interested, the due diligence will begin shortly, and an allocation is right around the corner.

Snap yourself back to reality. The fact is, that allocation may not come in for nine months, eighteen months, or even at all. That's the name of the game. However, you can improve the odds if you nurture the marketing process.

Phone canvassing is not just about calling new prospects—it is also about establishing professional relationships and maintaining an ongoing dialogue with existing contacts. Keep in mind that although an investor may not want to make an allocation in the next year or even two years, it never hurts to connect, because you never know when that investor could introduce you to someone who does want to do business with you.

The type of follow-up you do will depend on your existing relationship with the investor, the level of his or her interest, and the circumstances surrounding your last conversation. Below are some scenarios and suggestions for handling your follow-up. It is important to establish a process that works for you, and to stick to that process, over and over. Consistency will keep you organized with your management of contacts and will keep you on task within your overall marketing campaign.

Before we describe the different scenarios, one point must be made very clear: every follow-up starts with, and cannot exist without, accurate and up-to-date contact information. No matter what the scenario, one of the most important things to do is to acquire and verify the investor's contact details. Get the investor's full name with the correct spelling, his or her title, direct line, and e-mail address also with correct spelling; a bad e-mail address is of no use.

Now for the scenarios.

If an investor expresses a high level of interest, a follow-up call or a meeting is due immediately. Try to schedule a conference call with your portfolio manager and his or her team as soon as possible. If you are in the same city, or within a few hours, plan a face-to-face meeting. If you haven't done it yet, make sure you send the investor all of the relevant fund documentation.

If an investor seems only somewhat interested, offer to put him on your distribution list (he may also request this on his own). This means a follow-up call is due sometime within the next few months. Find out the best time of day to reach him and schedule a follow-up call. Enter the day and time in Outlook, your Blackberry, or whatever you use for your contact management system. Also find out if the investor will be in your area in the near future, or if he is attending any conferences near you. Even though the interest level is only moderate, never miss an opportunity to meet face-to-face.

If the investor seems to have very little interest, or none at all, make sure to find out why, because this will determine your next course of action. Is it your strategy? Then she's probably not a good person to follow up with at all. Maybe she has an interest in your strategy but is not keen on some of the fund terms or the investment style? Again, she's probably not a good person to follow up with, unless there are some dramatic changes in the fund's management. Make note of what the investor said, so that you don't spam her with e-mail in the future. Respect her point of view and don't push it. If you do, it will reflect poorly on you and, besides, it's a waste of time.

Does the investor have an interest in your strategy but is not impressed with your fund's performance or assets under management? Offer to check back in a few months with an update on performance numbers and assets (hopefully, both will be up). Is there mild interest, though little intent to invest in your strategy in the near term? Send a follow up e-mail, and offer to check back within three to six months.

The type of follow-up required will depend on the investor's level of interest and your existing relationship with the investor. Stay organized. Keep detailed notes about your conversations and your progress with certain investors. Be smart. Don't push something on someone who doesn't have an interest. Spend your time on those who are interested and on reaching out to brand new prospects.

The Recap

Phone canvassing is an effective way to reach investors—when done right. So train hard, know your targets, and focus on the task. That said, remember that it's also a numbers game. It will take time and many calls to make the right connection. The money is out there. You just have to find it.

RENEE ASTPHAN, *one of the founding members of BHA, manages a team of research analysts and writes for the* BHA Investor Monitor *and* BHA Quarterly Research Report. *Renee is responsible for all BHA client statistics and tracks all client subscriptions for trial and contract*

renewals. She also assists with the training and development of interns. Renee graduated from Ithaca College with a Bachelor of Science in Sport Management.

CT MCLEAN *is Senior Research Manager at BHA and directs the overall path of the research team.* CT *manages major strategic client accounts, assists with the training and development of interns and new employees, and writes extensively for the* BHA Investor Monitor *and* BHA Quarterly Research Report. *Prior to joining BHA in January 2008, CT was a Senior Fund Accountant at State Street Bank & Trust, working primarily with institutional money-market mutual funds. CT received a Bachelor of Arts degree in Business Management from Bryant University.*

Thirty-One Tips for Effective Marketing

Dennis Ford

I hope you are enjoying *The Fund Manager's Marketing Manifesto*. We've covered a lot of ground, so it's time to take a break. Grab a snack, put your feet up, and let me entertain you with an illustrated guide to the finer points of marketing. It's a little bit of my philosophy interspersed with some methodology and tactics.

Think of this as your cheat sheet—something to peek at before you get on a conference call or head into a face-to-face meeting. It's also a good way to stay in tune with your inner marketer. Marketing is a simple process, yet sometimes it's hard to stay focused amid the hustle and bustle. These general rules will help, if you keep them in the front of your brain at all times. So without further ado, let's get started.

1. Have a Good Attitude

Repeat after me: it is OK to laugh at ourselves and the predicaments we find ourselves in. It is your attitude that will make you or break you every single second of every single day. Wake up with a good attitude and the world just works right. Wake up with a bad attitude and the sky is falling and the earth is moving under your feet. Keep your attitude adjusted. Be positive. Be upbeat. Be optimistic. The alternative is not for the faint of heart!

2. Get Organized Already!

Something that promotes a good spirit is being organized. We all need to keep track of tasks and contacts, and make reporting our progress easier.

Unfortunately, many marketers spend inordinate amounts of time getting organized. Some invest in multiple software programs. Others read every self-help book that extols a new-fangled theory or method. Some are true in their pursuit of enlightenment; others are simply procrastinating. Either way, though, too much time on this is a waste of precious hours. You've got targets to call and a pipeline to fill. For the love of Pete, do not let self-help turn into an act of self-mutilation!

3. Teamwork Gets You Where You Need to Go

There will be days when you feel like a one-man SWAT team and your inner Rambo is ready to take the hill. Don't go it alone. It really takes teamwork—in the beginning, in the middle, and at the end—to win an allocation. So build your team and practice with your team, for when the game is afoot, you will surely need them.

4. Be You

A frequent barrier to effective marketing is self-image. When investors were coming over the transom, it was all about making hay when the sun shined. When the situation changed and marketers realized they had to go outbound, the stigma of selling crept into many a marketer's psyche. Will the firm look bad if we go outbound? Will I look desperate by aggressively marketing my fund? Is an outbound marketer more like a salesperson? Egad! What has become of me?

Stop that, right now. Be who you are: a marketer. Whether you do inbound or outbound marketing makes no difference. What's important is that your efforts are keeping your firm afloat and in good stead. There's no shame in that. So be proud of who you are. Don't try to hide.

Now that I have gotten you to accept who you are and what you do, you can fire your psychiatrist.

5. Protect Your #1 Asset—You!

You can't be successful unless you're feeling fit and on top of your game. The world you inhabit is stressful. You need to keep your mind and body in shape to deal with the stress. I am a big believer in working out three times a week. You, too, should make a point to get into a regular program. Pronto!

6. Ya Gotta Believe!

We have covered attitude, organization, teamwork, self-image, and of course, de-stressing and staying in shape. All this gets topped off with the concept of *believing*. You must believe you can raise capital for your fund.

True and earnest belief is as important as a strong work ethic. We all know folks who have the odds stacked against them, who don't seem to have a blessed chance in the world, yet they have goals so big that you wonder if they're right in the head. Then they succeed—they fly to the moon, make their millions, win the World Series (case in point: the Red Sox in 2004)—and everyone is amazed. Is it a fluke? No, it's believing!

7. Who's Who in the Zoo

Diligence and hard work are musts. That goes without saying. You also need to be savvy and understand all the players on your team and all the players at your prospects. There are no two ways about this. You need to figure out who's who in the zoo.

8. Stick with Your Program

Speaking of those inside and outside your firm, make sure you spend your time with people who add to your productivity. It is easy to let folks distract you from your mission. It is easy team up with colleagues who don't have the drive and motivation that you need to have. Such associations will derail you. Shun those who do not share your goals.

9. Respect Your Admins

Now let's talk about the administrative and support staff in your life. They can make you or break you. In fact, the power in most companies lies with the admins. So treat them well and show them the respect they deserve. If you don't, you might as well take that long walk to nowhere, because that is where you will wind up if you fail to grok the admin quotient.

10. You're the Maestro of Your Reality

By now you can probably see where I'm headed. It is you who must be the conductor of your orchestra. You are the person with the baton in hand, and it is up to you to get the orchestra ready for prime time. Everyone is watching you. Everyone awaits your signal. Once you start the performance, you can't miss a beat.

11. Sweat the Small Stuff

Although you may be directing the show, you also have to be aware of the details. There is a saying that the devil is in the details, and it's true. Pay attention to the details at every point in the allocation cycle. If you do not worry about the "little things," they will get you in the end and sink your ship. Be a sleuth, be a worrier, sweat the small stuff. Securing an allocation is all about taking care of all the details.

12. Call 'Em as You See 'Em

Securing an allocation is also about doing the right thing. You are the arbitrator of what is right and what is wrong. You and you alone have to make the call. You must summon your integrity and strength and call it like you see it. So many horror stories could be avoided if someone would only blow the whistle and lay down the rules of engagement.

13. A Fit Is a Fit

Another thing to keep in mind is the all-important concept of "fit." Develop an investor profile and then go after investors who fit that profile. This saves time on both sides of the table. Do not busy yourself trying to jam square pegs into round holes. A fit is a fit. If not, move on.

14. Connect the Dots

The universe of marketing is all about collecting data points and analyzing them to gain insight and an edge. This is basic Dot Connecting 101. The marketer who connects the dots the quickest will find the straightest path to cash. This means gathering clues from your work, your colleagues, and the marketplace and then connecting the dots to see a picture of how you can be successful.

15. Dial in Your Audience

The goal of a good marketer is to find investor targets that are a good fit. This requires creating an investor profile. Think about it. How can you go out into the alternative universe if you do not know who you are looking for? Take the time and create a crisp and cogent investor profile. Once you do, you'll see how easy it is to find targets.

16. Focus on Good Qualified Leads

One of the conundrums for most marketers is sticking with the investor profile that fits their fund and strategy. They compile lists and buy databases of all the alternative institutional investors (there are only about 50,000 of them on the planet), but they don't vet the leads. You must divide the targets into categories, and be very rigid about who is NOT a fit and who you will NOT pursue. Going after an investor who is not a fit is a waste of time for both parties.

17. Keep Your Cool

Many times you have to double your efforts to identify and produce good prospects. Having a bunch of leads on your desk or in your database that are not a fit and not qualified can get you in a fix pretty quickly. When you know you are short of good qualified leads, some marketers fall down the desperation rat hole. They get fearful, start to lose their cool, and forget to match targets against their investor profiles. They start e-mailing and calling randomly. AVOID DESPERATION.

18. Be Tactical on Your Trips

Remember, looking for prospective investors can be done in a mellow state with a preplanned strategy. Look at sections of your geographic turf as a prospect mall. Like all malls, there are probably three to five anchors (big prospects), the secondary players, and some outliers. So if you are calling on a large pension fund, figure out which family offices and other small investors are nearby. There is nothing wrong with killing two birds with one stone.

19. Seek and You Shall Find

One of the keys to effective prospecting is taking the time to really vet your territory. This means leaving no stone unturned. It is hard work, but it will pay off, because the harder you work the more prospects you will turn up.

20. Take Your Managing Partner on the Road

After you have identified your target group of investors, you need to organize conference calls and face-to-face meetings. For these you'll need the managing partner. Alert the managing partner to the importance of these calls and meetings and his or her participation. There's no way around this one.

21. Answer All Questions

When you get out on the road and
in front of alternative investors
who have mandates for your type
of fund and strategy, then you are
beginning the process. You are
presenting your fund and answering questions.

Answering questions is a BIG
part of the cycle. You must be the
one who knows the questions
investors will ask and knows how
to prepare your team to provide
the answers.

22. Find the One with the Keys

Once you find a good fit, you have to map it. One of the folks you need
to identify is the gatekeeper. The gatekeeper is the one in the organization who decides who will get in and who will be kept out. The gatekeeper makes sure that everyone gets the message: "If an outsider
surfaces, send them unto me."

23. No Belly Bumping

Here is a topic to ponder. Belly bumping! A big issue in the industry is ego. Let's face it, there is a lot of intellectual firepower in the alternative arena and some folks like to think of themselves as the smartest guys in the room, the cream of the crop, the raconteur bons vivants.

The issue with these fair-haired ones is that they tend to enjoy flaunting their intellect—sometimes at the wrong time. So when you drag your managing partner out the door to make an investor presentation, show him or her this cartoon and say, "Please, please, please, no belly bumping today."

24. Find a Navigator

As a matter of fact, the managing partner's marching orders should be to try to identify the navigator and cultivate a relationship with him or her. The navigator is the person on the other side of the table who has

some skin in the game. The navigator knows the firm well and will be able to guide you through the unfamiliar territory that you have to navigate to engage in a successful dialogue. The navigator is your inside go-to person. Most marketers who win allocations have taken the time to map the players who have participated in creating the mandate, and they have uncovered the gatekeeper and the navigator.

25. Hit the Reset Button

There are many players who come in and out of the picture during the course of the allocation cycle. It is imperative that you keep tabs on all of them. As a matter of fact, any time a new player comes into the fray, it is imperative to hit the reset button, start from the top, and go back to square one. Let them know who you are and why you are here. The most important aspect of marketing is keeping everyone in context, constantly. It is a daunting task, but and it makes all the difference in the world.

26. Good Things Come to Those Who Work Hard

If you can keep all of the points I've mentioned in the front of your brain, then a dialogue will start with the investor. The phone will be ringing, the e-mails will be coming in, there will be meetings to schedule, and you will be in what I like to call "the mix." This is truly the most fun part for a marketer.

27. Hang in There Until the Last Question Is Answered

It is precisely at this time when the marketer needs to be vigilant. This means being aware of any outstanding issues. I have a theory that when the last question is answered to the investor's satisfaction, then an allocation is just around the corner.

28. Patience Is Suffering

Just before the allocation, however, beware of the dead zone. The dead zone is that place in time when everything that has to be done is done, and now you wait. Depending on the category of investors and the length of their allocation cycle, this can be inordinately torturous. But this is how it is with allocation sign-offs in the alternative arena. You must learn to suffer gladly! I mean, you really have no choice. If you have done your job and all is right with the world, then inflows will be forthcoming.

29. Remember to Nurture Your Investor Prospects

There is inevitably a dead zone in every allocation cycle, but if you have been doing the right things throughout the process and caring for the opportunity, then all will be fine.

When in the dead zone, do not panic and do not overreact. Be respectful of the investor's time. Go about your business of cultivating the next potential investor. There is no option but to keep busy.

30. Have Faith and the Cash Will Come

Eventually, the phone will ring, the fax machine will kick into gear, or the bank account will show a wire transfer, and you will have secured an allocation!

31. Know When to Stop Marketing

At this point, it's critical to remember the golden rule: when you're done, you're done. Cease and desist with the pomp and circumstance. When you have secured an allocation from an investor, stop marketing to them. Your job is done.

Now, back to the business of marketing. I hope you enjoyed this brief intermission.

Developing Relationships on the Campaign Trail

CHAPTER 7

How to Organize and Execute a Road Trip

Jennifer Martin and Micah Jacobs

How hard could it be to plan a road trip? If you're like most managers, that's probably what you're thinking. Make a few calls, set up a time, book a flight, gather some slides, and you're done.

If that's your approach, then we're willing to bet that you've sat through more than a few mercy meetings. You know what we mean. Prospects agree to meet with you not because they are interested in your product, but because they are too kind to say no, were strong-armed into it, feel obliged because you were referred to them, or thought they would do you a favor.

You've also probably been in meetings where it's unclear who's who and why they're there, junior guys are interviewing senior guys, hyperactive portfolio managers are overwhelming mild-mannered investment advisors, and prospects are expecting to gather information, while managers are expecting an allocation. Then, of course, there are the meetings that take you half-way around the world when there's business right in your own backyard.

If you're tired of frustrating and fruitless road trips, here's the good news: there is a better way. It takes some time and effort, but having planned some 700 meetings, we can safely say that you'll have much more effective meetings. You'll meet with investors who are likely fits for your strategy, who are ready to ask questions and listen to your answers, and who are ready to go to the next step at the end of the meeting.

Many of our clients have had trouble seeing the value of road trips. When we began working with them, they were resistant to the notion, and told us that they'd probably do only one a year. Now, we're often still planning one when they're asking about the next one. We asked one client recently what changed his mind. He said, "It's simple. The way you organize road trips works!"

So read on. Once you know the ins and outs, you'll be able to execute more effective road trips and reap the benefits.

A road trip is one of the first steps in building a relationship with a potential investor. It allows you and your prospect to meet face to face and begin to develop a personal connection. It also lets you get a read (for better or for worse) of the person you want to do business with. Is he all business or the friendly type? Does he get right to the point or take some time to get to know you? Is he enthusiastic or cautious? You only have to be in front of a prospect for a few minutes to pick up a wealth of information that will help you get off on the right foot and develop a long-lasting association.

Much of this information is conveyed by a prospect's facial expressions and mannerisms and cannot be gleaned over the phone. In fact, having a phone conversation is often only steps above exchanging e-mail, where, as we all know, things are constantly lost in translation. Was he being serious? He must have been joking . . . or was he? Especially when you're speaking with someone for the first time, it can be hard to be sure what was meant.

Some marketers are naturals at reading people. For others it comes with experience. But that's good news, because now you know that the more you do it, the better you'll get.

Another reason it is helpful to go on the road and meet with prospects in person is that you're able to see the inner workings of the organization. How many employees it has, the way they interact with each other, and the chain of command all influence how quickly or slowly things get done and, therefore, are key to the allocation process.

As important as it is for you to understand the value of road trips, it is even more important that your managing partner understands their value, and that he or she is aligned with you. The powers that be do not always understand the marketing process. They may not grasp the importance of building relationships or that it must be done in person. You must make them see this. You also must make them understand that they need to be on the road as well. They are your firepower. Although you may pitch the product well, having the man behind the curtain with you to explain the ins and outs of the strategy is compelling.

Having everyone fully understand the importance of road trips will also make your job easier, as you will be allowed—even encouraged— to be on the road and in front of prospects more often. If you get push-back, show your statistics on the number of clients that are the direct result of road trips. Then show the total amount of assets raised from these clients. After all, that's what it always comes down to!

Did you know that your budget is better spent on road trips than on conferences? Chances are neither does anyone else in your firm. But it's true. At many conferences, the vast majority of attendees are other fund managers. Another large percentage are service providers who are attending in hopes of selling you their services. Of the investors who are looking to allocate capital, many will not be a fit for you or you will not be a fit for them. Some will have no interest in your strategy, others will be allocating below your minimums, and still others will want to make allocations that are too high. If you are lucky enough to find a few potential investors, having a meaningful dialogue is difficult, as you are competing with a number of other fund managers who are fighting for the same investors' attention. By contrast, on a road trip, you are in control. You are meeting with your target audience, who also wants to meet with you.

After you have convinced your team that the road is where you need to be, develop the right attitude and get excited about the opportunity to connect with your prospects face to face.

Determining Your Destination

To have a successful road trip, you must be organized, and you must do your homework. Deciding your destination is the first step.

Every successful marketer has an active hit list that he or she constantly adds names to, deletes names from, and mines every single day. It comprises your top prospects, which may include some low-hanging fruit. These are the prospects with whom you've had the most dialogue and the best relationships. They are the investors who are most likely to take a meeting with you while you are in town. Your hit list, then, is the best source of names to research when planning a road trip. Review it and ask yourself these questions: How concentrated are my top 10 prospects? Are they all in the same area? Can I plan a road trip based on these investors?

It's important to start planning a road trip at least a month in advance, so you have time to mine your hit list and figure out where the most demand is for your type of fund. If it's the United States, is it the West Coast, the Midwest, or the East Coast? Is it London? Maybe it's Switzerland. Then go where the market is telling you to go, which is wherever you can get the most meetings for a weeklong trip.

After screening your hit list for the top prospects, you'll probably have one to three places to visit. Next, think about who you have the best relationships with in these areas and how you can leverage them into additional meetings. Can someone make an introduction? How about a referral? By using your contacts, you will be able to use your time and travel dollars most effectively.

Additionally, figure out what else is going on in those areas. Is there an important conference or another industry event? If so, perhaps other prospects from other areas will be in town. Think broadly. Too often, marketers have tunnel vision. They focus only on their list. Rather, as you plan your itinerary—and even while you're traveling—always be thinking out of the box and connecting the dots so you get the most out of your trip.

After determining the locations and top prospects to visit, identify the look-alikes, followed by secondary targets. For example, if the majority of your top prospects are family offices, then you should also target small pensions and endowments, since these institutions are very similar in size, as are their decision-making processes. Secondary targets in this case would be funds of funds. Although their money might not be as sticky as that of a family office, funds of funds usually make decisions more quickly than institutions. Use meetings with look-alikes and secondary targets to fill the gaps between meetings with your top prospects.

If you don't have time to research and compile a list of look-alikes and secondary targets in the areas you're visiting, you may want to buy a list. There are many companies that sell contact lists at various price points. When evaluating and comparing such lists, the most important thing to look for is the freshness of the data. Data usually comes in two states: out of date and *very* out of date. There's nothing worse than buying a list of contacts, only to find that half of the phone numbers and e-mail addresses are wrong because the information is rarely updated. Do your research and make sure to buy a *fresh* list.

Contacting Prospects

Now that you have a game plan of where you are traveling, who to target, and a list of qualified prospects, the best way to begin contacting them is by e-mail. At least two or three weeks before your trip, send out an introductory e-mail with the dates of travel and a request for a meeting in the subject line. For example, "Joe Smith, CEO of Hot Hedge Fund Company, Request for Meeting in London June 1–8." Investors are inundated by hundreds of e-mails each week, so make sure yours is the one they open.

As noted in a previous chapter, the body of the e-mail should be brief. We suggest leading with your fund's most compelling attribute. In the following paragraphs, highlight those things that set your firm apart from others. This e-mail is the first introduction of your firm, and your first shot at getting a meeting, so make sure it stands out and gets your value proposition across quickly.

After you send the e-mail, track not only those prospects who are interested in a meeting, but also those who are not. A few days after you've sent this e-mail, you will want to send a follow-up to generate more meetings—and you don't want to send the second e-mail to someone who has already declined. That can be a quick way to lose your credibility as well as your chance to meet with that person in the future. So carefully track and delete the names of prospects who have responded.

Three to five days after your first e-mail, send a follow-up e-mail indicating in the subject line that this is your second attempt: "2nd Attempt: Joe Smith, CEO of Hot Hedge Fund Company, Request for Meeting in London June 1–8." Keep the body of the e-mail the same as it was in the initial e-mail, but add a sentence or two acknowledging that you have already reached out and are following up because you haven't heard back. As mentioned in an earlier chapter, the second attempt tends to produce more results than the initial one. Using "2nd Attempt" in the subject catches prospects' attention. In addition, as the date gets closer, there is more of a sense of urgency.

Between the first and second e-mails, be sure to canvass your targeted list by phone. In particular, call those who said they could not meet because they were traveling during your visit and those who did not say why they couldn't meet with you. Your goal is to turn these nos into yeses for conference calls or meetings at a later date.

Other responses may be vague and suggest that a person is not interested, but they may have been written in haste and the prospect may genuinely regret that he or she will be unavailable during your trip. Getting him or her on the phone is the only way to determine which it is.

Finally, if prospects tell you to contact them the next time you're in the area, don't let them get away that easily. Ask them to put something on the calendar now. Don't wait until your next trip is on the horizon and hope they remember what they said.

Scheduling Meetings

Your targeted e-mails have been successful and several prospects have responded favorably. Do not simply send back confirmation e-mails scheduling a date and time and move on. Pick up the phone and try to learn as much about both the contact and the firm as you can. For example, make sure he or she is indeed the correct person you should be meeting with. We have often followed up with prospects only to find out that it would make more sense on both sides to meet with someone else.

Also ask prospects if they have any questions prior to the meeting. When they read the e-mail, did any questions come to mind? This will help you to gauge investors' interest and avoid "mercy meetings." Many people will meet with you simply because you or someone else has asked them to. Although it is impossible to avoid this sort of thing entirely, speaking with the prospects prior to the meeting will give you a better feel for who is real. Ask a lot of questions, and try to figure out their investment timeline. Let them know that you don't want to waste their time. The goal is to have a compelling dialogue and see where the dots connect before the face-to-face meeting.

You've e-mailed twice, and some prospects have still not responded. This is when you start pounding the phones. Since you've already reached out with e-mail, there is no point in leaving voice mail; rather, keep calling until you get them on the line. In all likelihood, the prospects you are trying to reach are busy, which is why they haven't gotten back to you in the first place.

If this doesn't work, try different tactics. Call before and after hours, or during the weekend when they may be in the office trying to catch up on their work. There will undoubtedly be a lot of these phone calls to make, so prioritize your time. Start with your top prospects, and then proceed to the look-alikes, and finally the secondary targets.

Depending on how much time you have, you may want to send out a third e-mail to your target list indicating in the subject line that this is your third and final attempt: "3rd Attempt: Joe Schmo, CEO of Hot Hedge Fund Company, Request for Meeting in London June 1–8." This tends not to yield as many results as the second attempt, but it still may add a few more meetings to your schedule and cover some of the contacts you may not have had time to call.

As you make calls, send e-mails, and schedule meetings, be aware of prospects' locations, as you want to maximize your time and spend as little of it as possible traveling between meetings. Then, prior to arrival, determine the distance between meetings, and how you will travel to each. Is it feasible to walk, or will a taxi or the subway be more efficient? In London, you may have to wait 15 minutes or longer to get a taxi, so the tube may be your best bet. In New York, finding a cab is usually easy; however, the ride from midtown to downtown could be a solid 45 minutes, depending on the time of day. In this case, sticking with the standard hour between meetings may not always work out. So plan your itinerary carefully.

Preparing for Meetings

Once you have your schedule in place and the logistics figured out, make sure to research the firms you're meeting with, making notes so you have the information at your fingertips. In addition to their backgrounds, study the organization charts and know the roles of the individuals who will be in attendance. You want to make sure that you're meeting with those who will be actively involved in the decision-making process.

Here's a tip: don't deduce prospects' roles from their titles. At one firm, an analyst could be one of many who provide information to the CIO and main decision maker. At another firm, an analyst could be the right hand to the powers that be; meeting with him or her could be your ticket to an allocation. The only way to be sure you are seeing the right folks is to do your homework.

In addition to ensuring you're meeting with the right people, knowing their roles can put the situation in context and give your pitch direction. For example, a managing director at a small family office has different wants and needs than his or her counterpart at a large corporate pension or insurance company. Try to determine in advance what these wants and needs are by researching your prospects' current investments. How many funds are they currently invested in? What are the strategies of these funds? What kinds of risk-return profiles are they offering?

Preparing for meetings also includes rehearsing your pitch and updating your marketing materials. Check that all fund performance numbers are current, all relevant employees are listed, and all addresses are correct. Also, prepare a list of questions that you intend to ask. This will help you to direct the conversation and show your interest in the firm.

If you're traveling with colleagues, make sure everyone knows which roles they're playing and that the SWAT team is armed and ready for the maneuvers. A road trip is a well-planned deployment, not a haphazard, spur-of-the–moment outing.

Finally, dress to impress—and don't forget your business cards.

Meeting Your Prospects

Road trips take a lot of planning and preparation, and it isn't until you're in meetings with prospects that you often appreciate the value of face-to-face communication. As you make your presentation, you can see all prospects' facial expressions and body language, which are crucial in gauging comprehension and interest. Are they confused when you explain the ins and outs of your strategy? Are they impressed when you mention your returns over the past five years? Receiving this real-time feedback lets you tailor your pitch on the fly. Do they have a question? Would they like you to review that last point? When you can see prospects' expressions, you can more easily direct the presentation to suit their needs.

Additionally, by meeting in person you usually have your prospects' full attention, which is not always the case during conference calls. On a call, it may seem as though you have the listeners' attention, but they could be checking their e-mail, doing work, or any number of other things. Unless you're face-to-face, it's hard to tell if they are interested or bored, if they are really following you or just saying "okay."

Admittedly, even when you're standing right in front of someone, you can't prevent him or her from daydreaming. But you can detect it and do something about it. We had a meeting with a prospect who began doodling on his notepad. He was obviously miles away and missing important points of our presentation. We realized that we needed to reiterate the value proposition quickly and in a more creative way, or cut our losses and end the meeting. We didn't waste any time. One of us stood up, went to the white board, and started illustrating our points. That got the prospect's attention.

So your meeting went well and it's winding up. Before it ends, always ask your prospects if they know of anyone else you should be speaking with while you're in the area. Many times they do, and now that they've met you, they will make a suggestion. That's another benefit of face-to-face meetings: prospects are more willing to refer to you. Remember, you should always be looking to connect the dots. And you should always be looking to increase your pipeline. For that, referrals are king!

Critiquing and Follow-Up

At the conclusion of every meeting, assess the meeting with your colleagues. What was the prospect's feedback on your fund or strategy? Were there any new questions or topics that came up? If so, should they be incorporated into your pitch for the next meeting? Were you talking to the right decision makers? Did they understand the value proposition or were they confused? It's important to circle up after each meeting to see what your colleagues' impressions are and to make sure you are all on the same page with the assessment.

Also have your colleagues provide feedback on your pitch. This is critical. Your pitch is one of the most important assets you possess as a marketer. The better it is, the more successful you will be. Ask your teammates if they thought the prospect understood the firm and what it does. Did they think the value of the fund's offering came across? Think of your pitch as a living, breathing organism that needs feedback to grow. Good pitches change, evolve, and thereby constantly improve.

Prompt follow-up with the prospect after the meeting is also critical. Are there questions that need to be answered? Materials or references that need to be sent? The more time that elapses between the meeting and the follow-up, the more apt you are to lose the investor's interest. If you promised to send information, send it as soon as possible. If your travel schedule does not allow you do to so, make sure you have help set up back at the office to do this for you.

The importance of follow-up is something to keep in mind while scheduling your meetings. You want to fill your schedule, but you also should have enough time in the day for post-meeting follow-up. You do not want a potential allocation to wither on the vine due to your failure to act. It is imperative that once you have a prospect's interest you continue the dialogue.

Looking Ahead

The overall goal of the introductory meeting is to develop a strong relationship with a prospect that leads to a second, third, or even more meetings. The fact is, the allocation has become—for good reasons—a lengthy process. Successive meetings are required before prospects will make an investment. However, for prospects to book a second meeting, you need to have a compelling story and compelling performance. For them to book a third, you must answer their questions to their satisfaction.

So as you work toward getting that next meeting, prepare yourself. Anticipate the questions your prospects will ask the way a great point guard anticipates stealing a pass. You need to think of the different angles their questions may take, and be ready with answers. Your ability to answer all their questions will be instrumental in developing a long-term relationship and being seriously considered for an allocation.

JENNIFER MARTIN is a Senior Account Executive with Brighton House Associates. Jen is responsible for new business development and account management for New York City and the surrounding region. Previously, Jen was a Research Analyst at BHA. In this position, she gathered mandate information from investors worldwide and per-

formed data analysis to spot current trends. She also wrote for the BHA Investor Monitor. Jen earned a BA in Economics from Assumption College.

MICAH JACOBS is Marketing Manager of Parker Point Capital, a wholly owned subsidiary of Brighton House Associates and a broker-dealer. Micah manages a team of account executives who work directly with hedge fund clients, helping them source investors. Prior to joining Parker Point Capital, Micah was a Research Manager at Brighton House Associates where he oversaw the procurement and vetting of data and contributed to the BHA Quarterly Research Report and the BHA Investor Monitor. Micah began his career at Apple in IT sales and later worked for Nucleus Research, where he performed IT-related financial research. He earned a BA from the University of Vermont and an MBA from the F.W. Olin Graduate School of Business at Babson College. Micah holds Series 7 and 63 licenses.

CHAPTER 8

The Value of Validating Your Fund's Market Position

Dan Phillips

In April 2010, the University of Massachusetts Boston launched the Entrepreneurship Center as part of the College of Management. It was the culmination of an effort that began almost two years earlier, although I've long been involved with the school.

Sixteen years ago, I began funding my own scholarship and mentoring program at UMass Boston; it was my way of giving back. At the time, I was at my second high-tech start-up. I would go on to spend my 25-year career on the executive teams of four venture-capital-backed software start-ups. They were all early-stage, before-revenue companies. Two of the companies went public, one was acquired by EMC, and the other was acquired by Dell. It was after this last acquisition that I became more involved with the school.

Looking back on my experience, I realized that these companies all followed the same growth pattern. They invented a product or service, developed a prototype, tested it in the market, received feedback, built the product, launched it, raised money, grew an organization, established distribution channels, and sold the product. And it was a cyclical process that kept evolving, not a linear one. I also realized these companies all followed the same basic principles of entrepreneurship, and these principles could be applied to other start-ups—in high-tech, as well as in other industries.

So for the past two years I've been leveraging this experience, along with my network of colleagues and contacts in the Boston-area start-up community, on behalf of UMass Boston. It began simply enough; I offered to be a guest lecturer on entrepreneurship. The sessions were well attended and afterwards, many students expressed an interest in working in high-tech start-ups. They asked if I could give them advice about how to get internships. I reached out to companies I knew and began matching students' interests with companies' needs.

I also became involved with the Venture Development Center, where I'm currently entrepreneur in residence. The VDC is a business incubator at UMass Boston that offers start-ups the mentoring, connections, talent, and infrastructure that's necessary to launch a successful business. I work with companies that have been accepted into the program, helping them develop their product and business plans, and guiding them from the idea stage through the prototyping, marketing, fundraising, and sales phases. Through the VDC I have been able to formalize my internship program, which continues to find paid internships for UMass Boston students with the best high-tech start-ups in Massachusetts.

At the VDC, entrepreneurs launch start-ups in a live environment with cash burning and the clock ticking. However, my experiences with students taught me that they needed a controlled and mentoring environment where they can practice launching their own start-up. That became the impetus for the Entrepreneurship Center.

As the founder and director of the Entrepreneurship Center, I developed the curriculum for a concentration in entrepreneurship as part of the MBA program in the College of Management. I also teach a core course. The Center has workshops and events that team mentors with students to help them work on launching their start-ups.

Although I didn't intend to do another start-up, the Entrepreneurship Center is just that. It took two years to invent, and now it is ready to enter the next phase. What I learned from building all these start-ups is that companies must evolve in order to launch products or ser-

vices that meet the market's needs and to remain relevant. Additionally, the evolutionary process is circular and iterative, not linear. It is something that must happen continually. And it is something in which everyone in the company must participate.

I've spent my career in start-ups—start-ups that continually evolved and reinvented themselves. The shortest start-up was five years before IPO or acquisition. In each case, the founders thought they had developed a solution to a problem. But when we went out into the market with our product, the market told us differently. Luckily, each time we listened and reinvented ourselves, which I came to realize was not only essential to our success but also healthy.

Companies often reinvent themselves because of a major shift or event in their industry or market. A new technology is making their product obsolete, for example. Or a competitor's manufacturing efficiencies are putting pressure on prices and erasing their margins. When a company realizes its survival is endangered, it usually begins to react. Sometimes it succeeds; sometimes it runs out of time.

The fact is, however, that every company should be listening to the market and reinventing itself on a continuous basis—not only at a time of crisis.

Alternative investment funds are now at a reinvention stage. The financial debacle took its toll on hedge funds, as well as private equity, real estate, and funds of funds. Many closed their doors. Whether you are a seasoned survivor or a manager who's just getting started, you must take a hard look at yourself and your market and figure out how and where you fit in the new environment.

Your Business Description

When I talk with most founders and ask them what their business is, it usually takes five or ten minutes for them to describe it. And when they're done, no one understands what they said except them.

This is not a tenable position. No matter what business you're in, no matter how complex it may be, you must find a way to explain it to those who ask. This requires testing: devising a succinct explanation, saying it to prospects and clients, and then watching their expressions and listening to their responses. Did certain words resonate more than others? Did you lose their attention halfway through? Did they ask good questions, or were they unsure of what to say next? Did only folks "in the business" get it?

You can tell if someone doesn't understand what you said. When that happens, take note and change the way you describe your business. The only way to arrive at a clear, crisp description is by saying it, revising it, and trying it again.

When you have it, continue to test it, continue to refine it—and continue to be willing to completely change it. Most folks think that once they have a description their market understands, they're set. The market is constantly evolving, however, and so should your business description. In fact, testing the business description is something that everyone in your firm should work on continually, every day, for the entire life cycle of the company.

Your Unique Value Proposition

After developing a business description, the next step is articulating your unique value proposition. Every firm and fund has to have something that's unique or special—a reason for institutions to invest. This is particularly true for small and emerging funds. In fact, the smaller and younger your fund, the more important it is to have a unique value proposition.

Typically when founders launch a company, they think they know their unique value proposition. Sometimes they're right. But it's amazing how often they are wrong.

A U.S.-based hedge fund was having difficulty raising capital. They had a top-performing quantitative fund that was getting them in many doors. Yet at the end of these meetings, the result was always the same:

the investors hesitated to take the next step. One day, after another unsuccessful meeting, an exasperated partner asked the investor why he had invited them in.

"Because we heard you had experienced traders."

"We do," replied the partner. "We have some of the best in our niche."

"Well you haven't told us about them," answered the investor.

The fund's pitchbook emphasized the young hot-shot traders at the firm, but the investors they were pitching were looking for experienced traders, folks who had been through some market ups and downs.

There is only one way to know if your unique value proposition is right or wrong: ask your prospects and clients. They will tell you why they're talking to you, and what you have that your competitors don't. Use this information to revise your value proposition. Then test it in the market, and see how others react.

One client may say he or she invested with you because you have experienced traders. Another may note that not only do you have experienced traders but also they are from well-respected companies. Still another may point out that some of your traders are from a well-known division of a company.

You get the point. Ask, refine, and ask again. Your value proposition should be as tight and precise as possible. Most firms that go through this process discover that their value proposition is not what they thought it was.

As you refine your value proposition, you must also go back and see if it changes your business description. Before this manager met with this investor, the firm described itself "as a global hedge fund that generates alpha by combining the latest technology with innovative investment approaches." After it became clear that prospective investors were more interested in their veteran traders than their innovative hot-shots, the firm changed its business description to "a global hedge fund manager that generates alpha using an experienced team and proven strategies."

In essence, a firm tests its business description, and it changes. Then the company tests its unique value proposition, and it changes, which in turn may alter the business description.

Your Market Definition

Defining your market is the process of identifying the target audience for your fund. Who is it most effective to market your fund to? Most companies think they have a very broad market—that they can market to everyone. This is never the case. Even large consumer-products companies don't target everyone. They have very large market segments, but they are segments nonetheless.

In addition to being unrealistic, thinking too broadly can cause practical problems. After test marketing a product, companies often find themselves trying to please all potential customers—usually by adding features—which can trigger a host of unintended consequences: the product becomes more complex and takes longer to develop, increasing production costs, limiting pricing flexibility, and delaying shipping. Companies often sacrifice their competitive lead bringing an expanded product to market, only to find months or years later that customers complain about the product's complexity and use a small fraction of its features.

Keep this in mind as you test market your fund and define the audience. As you collect more and more data, it may seem like your market is getting broader and broader. Many types of prospects may tell you they would invest in your fund. And your instinct is to accommodate them. However, you need to do the exact opposite. Rather than expand your market, make it narrower and narrower. Let me give you an example.

Asia's promising growth has been attracting many investors. It also has been attracting a lot of hedge funds. Large global companies, as well as a host of start-ups, have opened offices in the region. The increasing number of funds caught a particular hedge fund by surprise. Although it had been in Asia for years, it was unsure how to compete in such a crowded market.

It took a look at its business. The firm had investors of all sizes and all types. It had some private investors, some institutions, and some funds of funds. Of the institutions, several were pension plans. It had some contacts in this area, so it decided to focus its efforts on these investors.

After a few months of cold calls and meetings, the partners were back at the drawing board. They had learned that they were too small for the largest government pension plans. From that they deduced that it would be equally hard to attract large corporate pensions. In the United States, they contacted some state pension plans, but found that many also considered them too small.

They looked again at their client list. They realized that the pension funds that invested with them tended to be those for larger municipalities and funds for police and firefighters. So, they decided to set a new target.

This time, their efforts were successful. It was not only easier to set up meetings with potential investors but also to close more business. Equally important, however, by zeroing in on the right market, they had found an advantage over the competition.

The moral is: the more precisely you define your market, the more successful you will be.

Of course, after you define your market, you should revisit your business description and value proposition. Can you more clearly describe your business now? Can you more accurately articulate your unique value proposition?

The Competition

You can gather a wealth of information by knowing who your competition is. But until you know exactly the market you're going after, your unique value proposition, and your business description, you can't determine who your competition is or perform any type of competitive analysis.

After you've refined those things, however, then you can get the lay of the land. What other funds are you competing with? What are their strengths and weaknesses? How do their funds stack up against yours? Can you complement them in some way? What can you learn from them? Who are their clients?

If, like the Asian hedge fund, you refine your market definition, it's much easier to identify competing funds, determine how you measure up, and decide how to position yourself in the marketplace.

Additionally, the more you study your competition, the more information you will have to refine your business description, your unique value proposition, and your market definition.

Your Fund

The next step is test marketing your fund. This means getting in front of your defined target audience, showing them the fund, explaining the features, and receiving feedback. You think you have a fund that addresses a need—now you must get confirmation.

Sometimes this takes hours and days of face-to-face meetings, asking a lot of questions—what they think of your fund, what's good and bad, what they would change—and listening closely to their feedback. During this time, you also must discover their biggest pain points.

Be forewarned. After spending hour after hour with your clients and prospects, it is highly likely that their feedback will significantly change what you think about your fund. That's the point of test marketing. It may be disappointing, but think of it this way: when you begin marketing your fund, you can be confident that you have something that the market wants.

There's another benefit to all this as well. By spending so much time in the field, you gain an enormous amount of knowledge. You come to understand the needs and requirements of prospects and clients like few others in your market and industry. You truly become an expert.

So, gathering detailed information on your clients' requirements usually changes your business description, your unique value proposition, and your market definition. It also changes your competitors. And it obviously changes your fund.

A Case Study: The Value of Testing

My last start-up was Silverback Technologies. When we began, we were a managed service provider, or MSP. That was the business description. What was unique about us was that from one location we would remotely solve the computer problems of many companies, and for less money than they could do it themselves.

Like most start-ups, we thought we had a very broad target market. After all, who doesn't have computer issues? We also thought our competitors were software vendors that sold high-end tools to companies so their IT folks could perform this service. Finally, we thought our business model was building a data center and staffing it with technology experts who would connect to companies remotely. Our infrastructure costs to build this service were high, but the end-user value and the fees prospects were willing to pay for this service were high as well.

As we went into the market, we learned that it was the really small companies that needed this type of service. However, these companies didn't only want someone to fix their problems remotely. They also wanted someone on site. Someone who could offer advice, suggest changes, sell them products, install them, and get everyone up and running. In short, they wanted a one-stop shop.

We couldn't cost-effectively build a company that offered remote and on-site service. In addition, there were companies that did this—hundreds of thousands, in fact. They were called value-added resellers, or VARs, and small companies were used to buying from them.

The VARs, it turned out, had a problem. The majority of their revenue came from selling hardware and software, which has low margins. Many were looking for a way to get into a higher margin business with recurring revenue.

We decided to reinvent ourselves. No longer would we be an MSP. Rather, we would become a software company that provides VARs with programs that enable them to become MSPs. We also would develop consulting and training services that would help the VARs become MSPs.

Test marketing our service changed our view of our business and our opportunity. As a result, we changed our business description, our value proposition, and our market definition. No longer were we targeting end-users. Now we pitched VARs that sold to end-users. Our competitors were no longer vendors that sold high-end tools. They were low-end VARs who wanted to expand on their own.

Our business model also changed. We didn't need a big data center or a large staff. Our costs were much lower. However, selling software meant less revenue per deal. So now we needed to close more deals.

The evolution of Silverback didn't stop there. Soon, we had a large and successful company. And because of our success, many competitors entered the market with cheap, low-cost alternatives to our product. They commoditized the market, and it became difficult to turn a profit unless one had millions of customers.

So once again we reinvented ourselves. We had a robust, scalable software platform that was head and shoulders above the products our competitors were offering. We decided to see if this was viewed as a competitive advantage in the market. We met with large strategic companies that had millions of customers, such as telcos and computer companies. Our plan was to be the platform these companies used to service their large customer bases. Dell was one such company. As we talked to them, various ideas surfaced—one of which was an offer to buy our company and integrate it into Dell's service offerings, and we accepted.

None of this—which took seven years, by the way—would have come to a successful conclusion had we not talked directly with customers every day and always asked who we were and what they needed.

A Mindset

Test marketing is a mindset. It's a mindset that must start at the top and involve the whole firm. Partners, traders, marketing folks, administrative assistants—everyone. You cannot assume that you understand the needs of prospects and clients. You can't be sure that what folks wanted yesterday they will still want tomorrow. You must ask them.

Then you must share this information with others in your firm. This will only happen, however, if you have a collaborative organizational structure and environment that enables and encourages employees to share what they learn, discuss it, and think about what other information it would be valuable to gather.

It's not always easy, but you also must empower your employees to make decisions and act on the information they learn. After twenty-five years and four start-ups, I've learned the value of employees who are willing to take the initiative. There's always more than one way to do something. So if you have people who are smart, creative, and want to take on tasks, let them. They will not only figure out how to execute the tasks, they will take them to the next level.

Could someone make a mistake? Yes, that will happen. But at least it will be an informed decision or a calculated risk. In fact, it's often better to respond relatively quickly to new market data than to sit on it. So let someone run with the ball. You will have many more wins than losses.

You may be wondering how much time this takes. Test marketing is not a task that you plan and execute. It's a continuous process that is embedded into every minute of your day. In the beginning, it may seem like it takes a lot of time and effort. However, after it becomes part of everyone's mindset, they'll hardly give it any thought at all. It will become second nature, which is as it should be.

DAN PHILLIPS is founder and director of the Entrepreneurship Center at the University of Massachusetts Boston. He is also entrepreneur in residence at the university's Venture Development Center. Prior to joining the university, Dan spent twenty-five years as an executive with four venture-capital-backed software companies. Two of these compa-

nies achieved successful initial public offerings on NASDAQ, and two were acquired by Fortune 200 companies. Dan was the COO of Concord Communications, which attained a market capitalization of $800 million. He also was the CEO of Silverback Technologies, which was acquired by Dell. Dan has funded his own scholarship and mentoring program at UMass Boston for the past sixteen years.

CHAPTER 9

Best Practices for a Successful Fundraising Campaign

Dennis Ford

As the person responsible for Brighton House's growth, I have spent the past four years studying how institutions invest and how managers fundraise. During this time, it became clear to me that some fund marketers are adroit at raising capital in almost any environment. I also noted that some marketers are living in the past and have yet to adapt their marketing tactics and strategies to the new fundraising environment. Others lack an overall, concrete picture of the evolving allocation process and how it works. As a result, for many marketers, their success rates at identifying new investors and securing fresh capital are at an all-time low.

Since the financial crisis, I've increasingly heard general partners and managing directors express frustration about raising capital. To a great extent, what they say is true: competition is fierce and fundraising is hard in this post-crisis environment. I couldn't help but think, though, that it would be much less difficult if they knew more about how to market their funds in the current environment. If they changed their old tactics, adjusted to the new realities of elongated allocation cycles, and used outbound marketing techniques, they'd be more successful.

So in this chapter, I combine my 25 years of experience selling and marketing with what I've learned from speaking with thousands of investors and managers, and provide you with a road map and some best practices for outbound marketing.

In previous chapters, we've talked about finding potential investors, so you can begin to build relationships that eventually lead to investment. The alternative arena is full of potential investors. Brighton House has identified 16 categories of alternative investors and about 50,000 institutional and private firms that allocate to alternative investments. Your job is to ferret out targets based on your firm's investor profile, identify them as good or bad, and then get them on or off your plate as fast as possible. A good target is one that has a chance of being a fit.

So, what's a fit? This is the obvious question for the marketer. You have a fit when a prospect has a real need for your fund, has done the analysis, decided on a specific investment strategy, and has a mandate to make the allocation. If a target passes this initial qualification test, SHAZAM, it becomes a prospect. It becomes a HOT prospect when the allocation time frame is relevant to your current monthly, quarterly, or annual fund raising goals.

Remember, nine to eighteen months is now the standard allocation time frame. This is based on the investor extensively researching the management team and watching the fund perform for two to three quarters before investing.

Identified

The first stage of the allocation process is what I call the "identification stage." It's the phase when a target investor surfaces, expresses an interest, shows some signs of life, and you officially identify him or her as a prospect. Ideally, such a potential investor has some kind of deadline outlined in a mandate. This is when you have a meeting or two and a dialogue starts to happen. When you have a prospect, you are in the game and playing for money, although your chances of turning a prospect into a client are only 10 percent at this stage. You are at the beginning of the pipeline, or "the pipe" as I like to call it.

The pipe is a way to measure the progress of a prospect or allocation. It's the antidote to fruitless and exasperating hoping-and-wishing meetings. If your company doesn't have a way to classify the status of your prospects, do WHATEVER IT TAKES to get everyone singing from the same hymnal. Get yourself and the executives in the same room. Start a dialogue. Outline what it takes to do an allocation. Have the managing partner and the powers that be buy off and agree that this is the new process of raising cash.

Next, decide how to classify prospects, so that they can create accurate fundraising forecasts. See the pattern? This is how you the marketer educates the rest of the company on how fundraising works. When this is done properly and everyone in the company understands what it takes to raise money, everyone's job becomes easier.

Typically, I consider prospects to be in MY personal pipeline when I have identified them as a prospect. Before that I call them noise. Prospects can fall out of my pipe at any time for any number of reasons, although if they reach the end, they exit as clients.

When you're in the identification stage, you're likely talking or meeting with the information gatherers or the gatekeepers. These two groups are part of the investor landscape, and you must meet with them to qualify a prospect and figure out if you have the makings for some inflow. However, you don't want to put a potential investor in the firm's pipeline until you have met with the navigators and decision makers and feel positive about the fit.

The Information Gatherers

Usually, the information gatherers are folks who are good at ferreting out information and understanding fund strategies. They don't necessarily know all the specifics, such as why they have been assigned a task, what the information will be used for, or when it will be used. Therefore, they can't answer our all-important marketer questions. All they know is they've been asked to use their analytical brains to gather and collect information on certain types of managers and their strategies.

Sometimes marketers try to make a meeting with an information gatherer more important or pivotal than it is; this is always a waste of time and effort. Recognize it as a simple information transaction. That's what it is! Provide the information in as nice a package as you can, and then go on your merry way. It is not an automatic prospect when you hand out some information. Maybe it's a target. Deal with it!

Having said that, you can't take anything for granted. You must probe to make sure the info gatherer really is a low-level person and not more than that. I remember a conversation I once had with an info gatherer when I was involved with a software technology company. I asked him what he was looking to do.

"Who, me? I'm just collecting some data on some stuff we're looking at."

"What stuff?" I asked.

"Oh, I'm trying to understand what companies are doing in this area and the products they have. Then I'll pass the info along to some folks in the company."

"What for?"

"We're trying to make some decisions, I guess."

"Well, who are you and what do you do?"

"Who, me? Oh! I'm the CTO of IBM's Life Sciences Group."

Bingo!

Keep in mind that the answer could have been that he was a student doing an internship. In fact, some info gatherers are interns rather than key players. A CEO asks the S.V.P. to identify the top ten vendors that market a specific product. The S.V.P. delegates the task to the V.P., who gives it to a department manager, who assigns it to an associate, who passes it on to an assistant, who gives it to the intern. That's corporate for you.

However, sometimes CEOs and other top-level executives are in a hurry and don't want to wait around for the information. They can do a Google search as quickly as the next guy and line up a couple of meetings. So ask who and why. You never know!

Open Sesame—The Gatekeepers

The gatekeepers keep you out or let you in. Most accomplish this task by making all fund manager roads lead to them. They tell the receptionists, administrators, and everyone that counts, "SEND THEM UNTO ME." Others are pulled into the game on an as-needed basis.

Let's say you are calling high, and you get through—you get the managing partner on the line. They refer you down the ladder to someone else, or days later, someone else calls you back. You're thinking, hmmm, maybe I will see some action here. This person is the gatekeeper.

The gatekeepers usually are the in-the-know folks, and part of their job description is to parse good things into the firm and turn away nuisances. For the most part, gatekeepers are easy to find, as they tend to be in the "front of the house" or within arm's reach of the executive suite. They usually are knowledgeable about the firm. They are easy to get by if you have something that makes sense, but they do not suffer fools gladly.

The gatekeeper is probably the first stop for your e-mails, phone calls, and pitchbooks. Maybe the investor is looking for an emerging markets hedge fund, and is not interested in long/short equity, managed futures, global macro, or any of the other 30 to 40 strategies that are out there. So the gatekeeper only lets the emerging markets managers through.

The gatekeepers are incredibly busy folks and besieged by marketers, so it's hard to get their attention. There are about 20,000 managers trying to get 50,000 alternative investors to invest in their funds. As a result, gatekeepers are inundated with hundreds of e-mails, phone calls, and pitch books a week. That's a lot of day-to-day noise.

To stand out, your best bet is to send the gatekeepers some crisp, timely information that you know they need. Of course, to know what they need, you have to do your homework. These are binary folks. You won't get by them with glad-handing and chicanery. But solid, concise, bottom-line rationale works well. Oops! There's that credibility thing again. (Although it never hurts to be friendly and personable, too.)

The gatekeepers are not going to give you a lot of opportunities to get into their companies. Your first attempt must be well thought out and well planned, and you must be organized. Before you contact them, for example, have an e-mail package ready to send as soon as you get off the phone. Before you meet with them, make sure you know your stuff. If you don't, bring someone with you who does. If you tell a gatekeeper that you want to bring one of your company's great folks to talk to him or her personally, most likely you'll get one of two reactions. The gatekeeper will volunteer to bring some of the firm's folks as well—or not. If not, then you know this gatekeeper's got clout.

Either way, get a meeting scheduled. Get in there! Use the gatekeeper to map the firm's players and how their process works. Of course, you should do your own map first.

Mapping a Company

There are various ways to map firms that make alternative investments. At one extreme are the marketers who approach it like a reconnaissance mission. They gather all the information they can find and comb through it before the big meeting. They do nothing short of an exhaustive analysis of the prospect, its peers (other possible leads), and the industry. At the other extreme are marketers who do just enough research to have a good idea of the prospect's specific investment category, and gather the rest through real-time, face-to-face dialogue.

There are many pros and cons to these two methods, and either one or a combination thereof will probably fit you. One advantage to the deep-dive, information-overload approach is that prospects perceive you as well informed, credible, and perceptive. This evokes respect and trust, which helps you forge solid relationships.

On the other hand, I've seen marketers who spend way too much time researching and not nearly enough on the phone or on the road.

And when they finally do talk with a prospect, they are so focused on verifying their data that they don't really hear what the prospect is saying.

Now, don't get me wrong. You must verify your data. Some marketers simply assume that the information they gathered up front is correct. They don't confirm it, and they pay the piper later on. All I'm saying is, don't let the data run the meeting.

The best approach is when the prospects talk and the marketers listen. They draw people out, read between the lines, verify what they hear, connect the dots, and ask and answer questions. It's an honest, real-time dialogue, which also garners respect and trust, and lays the foundation of a good relationship. It also maximizes the amount of time they spend in contact with prospects. Unfortunately, many marketers believe themselves to be faster on their feet than they really are, and they misconstrue less prep for no prep, leading to disastrous results.

It's hard to gauge how much up-front time you should spend, but good marketers find a happy middle ground between these two extremes. Here's a tip: the amount of time should be determined by how familiar you already are with the prospect and the importance of the call.

First Impressions

So you are meeting the information gatherer or gatekeeper and starting a dialogue. This is a critical point. During the first few meetings, prospects form an impression of you and your company that sticks with them and becomes their long-term view. Don't be a glad-hander or pushy marketer. Also, know the rules. Many alternative investors consider all conventional sales tactics off limits, because of the changing regulatory environment. Make sure you know the SEC regulations before you get in front of an investor.

To lay the foundation for an honest dialogue with your prospects, first, know your fund. Then listen to their issues, ask them questions, answer their questions, and show them that you, your team, and your company want them to understand how this relationship can be a success for both parties. If you do this, they will see you as a credible marketer.

The process of qualifying a prospect is extremely helpful here. During a meeting, you confirm your map of the company, verify that there is a mandate and timeline, establish an outline of the allocation process, discover a few pain points, find out if they're talking to your competitors, and zero in on who will be the ultimate navigator of the process. You draw the prospect out, open up a dialogue, and have an honest exchange of information, and everyone gets comfortable.

Hey! Here's a notion for your marketer head. Every time you call on a prospect—whether it's an information gatherer, gatekeeper, or even a decision maker—look at it like you are going to get to know a new person, not secure an allocation. You ask about this and that, and you tell them what you are up to and what you are trying to do.

I always go into meetings being the friendly, knowledgeable, prepared, and genuinely caring marketer that I am. I want prospects to form the impression that this guy and this company are in the know. I want prospects to say thanks for a great meeting, we learned a lot, and we look forward to working with you. I want to say the same back.

One way I do this is by being a color commentator, just like the sports folks on TV. Their value is providing insight into what's happening at any given moment during a game. When you think about it, this is something marketers can do easily. In the past four years, I have talked to more than a thousand fund managers, from emerging to multibillion-dollar funds, and I have learned lots. If you have been in an industry or territory for a while, you know all the key players and who's buying what from whom. You know who's doing well, who isn't, who has the latest and greatest, and who's playing catch up.

Such knowledge is fascinating and interesting to prospective investors. Synthesize and deliver it in a lucid and cogent way, and you can enhance your credibility, not to mention be someone they like to talk to. You, too, can be a pundit, a bon vivant raconteur, or an industry analyst—just know your stuff! Most important, know the rules of the road (SEC guidelines) when it comes to marketing your fund.

It's Only the Beginning

During the indentification stage, a picture begins to emerge, a relationship forms, and things seem off to a great start. This is where many a marketer is led astray, and sees an allocation when there really isn't one or shouldn't be one.

Let's face it. Marketers feel pressure to put something on their forecast. They get overanxious to turn a target into a prospect, slip into the *Marketer's Magical Reality,* and are off in la-la land. They begin to see things that aren't there, try to force a fit, or use every skill they have to push along something they shouldn't. Don't do that!

Listen to your gut. Think back to an allocation that came together as it should have. Remember the circumstances that gave you confidence, and the moment you knew you could honestly say to yourself, "They will be a client. They just don't know it yet." Then stay in the real world. Opportunities change direction, get postponed, stumble and fall off a cliff, lie there, or out and out die. They are very tricky creatures. They prey upon your optimistic nature. They get you in a fix.

That is why it's imperative to concentrate really hard on the good prospects and 86 the bad ones, pronto! It is also the reason to set everyone's expectations. Let them know that a potential allocation is ready for the forecast only when it's truly at the fifty-fifty stage. Those are better odds from a marketer's standpoint, and therefore can be added into a forecast with the proper caveats.

Movin' Down the Pipe—In Play

After initially qualifying a prospect, the next step is to develop a relationship. A good marketer recognizes this, and doesn't rush, overwhelm, or hassle the prospect, no matter how much pressure is being exerted by those higher up the food chain.

The fact is, allocations take time, especially since the timeline is longer than it used to be. It is, at a minimum, nine to eighteeen months and can easily get stretched out further. That's why it's important to have many irons in the fire. You'll get killed if all you do is worry and bother a few prospects. You must learn to say, let's wait! Let's give them some time! Let's not overwhelm the prospects with our overzealous desire to get an allocation. Hold off, take a deep breath, chill, be calm, relax.

Don't smother or tick off a prospect because you have ants in your pants. Take the time to develop relationships with the right folks. The right folks at this stage are the evaluators, the navigators, and the recommenders.

The Evaluators

When the evaluators enter the picture, the game is afoot! Here's the skinny: the evaluators are the ones who roll up their sleeves and look closely at your fund. This means hearing your pitch, meeting the founders and executive team, and then monitoring the fund's performance quarter to quarter.

They also watch how the fund executives react when they beat their predictions, and how they act when they miss. These issues are at the forefront of investors' minds today. Their new modus operandi is to watch and wait, validate performance, and get to know the executive team. Liquidity and transparency are the new buzz words. You and your firm need to be ready with cogent answers and commentary for the latest shift in investor sentiment.

It is easy to do a good job with evaluators and just as easy to foul it up. I have seen countless marketers let their counterparts in a fund group handle the due diligence phase. They go about their business thinking all will be fine. Don't be stupid. Weird things can happen. What you thought would be a slam-dunk evaluation turns into a full-blown firestorm over the most inane and innocuous things. A run-of-the-mill meeting is suddenly dominated by people who love to belly bump each other over how smart or knowledgeable they are regarding a strategy or the current and future state of the market.

Good marketers know to be ever vigilant during this process. They leave nothing, and I mean absolutely nothing, to chance. If the sparks start to fly, they are there to put out the fire and calm the group.

Another thing to avoid at all costs during evaluation meetings: allowing folks to take each other down rat holes. It happens all the time. Two people are off topic and heading straight into never-never land. A good marketer keeps the group focused and never gets involved in the chase.

The best way to start an evaluation meeting is to set the stage or create the context for the evaluation. Keep it simple. First, go over the agenda for the meeting, making sure folks agree with it, know why they're here, and understand what they're trying to accomplish. Then take them through it, step by step.

Part of your agenda should be to present your fund, and highlight the synergies between it and their mandate. As you explain your fund's strategy, your understanding of their mandate, and how you may fulfill their requirements, you should be seeing some sort of positive feedback from your audience. They may be smiling, voicing their agreement, or simply nodding—all good signs. If there's disagreement, smirks, or scowls—or worse, no reaction whatsoever—you are in trouble. Step in fast—and I mean pronto.

Start with some open questions: "Mr. Evaluator, are we showing you what you want to see? Did you expect something else? Did we misunderstand what you are looking for or what your needs are? I'm sensing a disconnect here. Are we disconnecting?"

Such direct, open, frank questions should be enough to elicit some feedback. Then you can adjust or regroup. However, never let the evaluation deteriorate without trying to understand why: "Mr. Evaluator, I feel we are heading south here. Please tell me why."

One of the mind-blowing aspects of marketing presentations is the shoulda-woulda-coulda phenomenon that occurs afterwards. You're in the car, restaurant, or back at the office after an investor presentation.

One by one, the team starts to dissect the meeting and participants: Do you think the investor understood our new strategy? Do you think he doubted our performance numbers? Do we know when and how the firm is planning to make the allocation?

All good questions THAT SHOULD HAVE BEEN ASKED DURING THE MEETING.

Do not waste a meeting with a prospect. If you have thoughts, questions, observations, or insights, speak up! Now's the time, while you're all together. Get it all out on the table. Point out any issues you see or perceive on their side or yours, and get them resolved. The alternative is catch-up mode: you ask for another meeting so you can address some open issues, or you track down the participants individually to clear things up. It's frustrating. It's time consuming. And, yes, sometimes it's necessary, though often it can be avoided.

Listen up! Evaluation meetings are good. Evaluations are necessary. No one is going to make an investment in a fund without evaluating it. From time to time, you'll hear fund executives encourage marketers to try to get around the long evaluation process. They believe evals slow down the process, that you could close allocations much more quickly if you didn't have to go through that step.

The fact is, evaluations are probably the most important part of the allocation process. It provides the investor with a hands-on look at your fund and an understanding of the management team.

The Navigators

At some point, as an allocation progresses through the pipe, the navigator surfaces. The navigator usually appears during the evaluation or recommendation stage, and is the one who has the most skin in the game. This person's success is riding on the outcome of the allocation—whether it be with you or your competitor.

The navigator is your go-to guy or gal, your sponsor, your new best friend, and the person you need to convince. Learning to identify the navigator is imperative. It is also tricky, as all the people you meet along the way may tell you that they are the navigator. They don't mean to mislead you. At that point in the process, they are the ones making the call. But you have to figure out who the real navigator is—the one who's going to guide you through to the end. This is one of the reasons why I mentioned earlier to always verify who you're talking to. Miss the navigator and you may miss your allocation.

The navigator is the one most closely associated with the reason this investor is evaluating your fund in the first place. This person may actually be the one who created the mandate and is responsible for picking the right manager. It is imperative that you build a solid relationship with the navigator.

The Recommenders

The recommenders are pivotal to the process—their opinions and recommendations really count. These folks surface every time, but they generally stay behind the scenes until they need to get involved.

The recommender is usually an executive who is tasked with scanning the market for fund managers who fit a specific investment need. When you meet with a recommender, you start talking more seriously and more in-depth about performance and risk. The recommenders are the folks who get an allocation tied up into a neat little package, with a bow on top.

If you get to the recommender you have a good shot at winning the allocation. The recommender will narrow his or her choices to a handful of managers, and you can bet all your competitors are still in the running. It's here that you, your fund, and your company all have a major bearing on who gets recommended to the decision maker.

A good marketer works on developing good relationships with *all* the folks in the investment process: those helping out at his company and those helping out at the investor's. But he or she gets as tight as possible with the recommender. The better the relationship, the easier it is to get the real scoop on what the issues are and how to address them.

Always keep in mind this simple fact: an allocation process starts out with a particular mandate, which is defined by a set of requirements. You have to understand the mandate requirements, and keep your eye on what is happening during the evaluation process. The marketer who stays on top of the nuances of the process usually wins because he or she is current and in context.

The Importance of Context

One reason so many opportunities get blown is lack of context. You know the moment: you're in a meeting trying to get some commitment that will move the process forward, when someone pipes up and says, "I thought it leaped tall buildings in a single bound." The managing partner's eyes dart over to you and you say, "Well, not exactly, but it's faster than a speeding bullet."

Before the words are even out of your mouth, you know that was the wrong answer. But what's the right one? Who is that guy? And why do you get the distinct feeling that your allocation is suddenly on the ropes?

I'll tell you. During the allocation process there are lots of meetings and lots of people moving in and out. It is hard to keep everyone on the same page, and this is the person that you missed. He has some wrong information. At this critical juncture, when you're looking to confirm that all's right with the world and the process, he's raising doubts.

Nothing can derail an allocation faster than a prospect with the wrong information. It may be about your fund, your company, the allocation parameters, their needs, their objectives, the fit, or any number of other things. It doesn't matter. It gets you off track.

This is why at the first sign of a change, rewind and start over. As soon as someone new comes in the room, give him or her a summary of your presentation so far. As soon as you move up a notch in the marketing process, present your fund from scratch. As soon as someone makes a statement or asks a question that could foul up the perception of your fund, jump in: "OK, Ms. Investor, let's take it from the top. Here's our fund. These are the needs you have outlined in your mandate. Now, is that a fit?"

This is not something you do just for the evaluators. It is something you must do every time someone comes into your orbit. Everyone you meet during every stage of the allocation process tends to start brainstorming, think of what-if scenarios, or just go into fantasy overdrive. Don't let anyone derail the process. Put everyone in context. THIS MEANS EVERY SINGLE PERSON EVERY SINGLE TIME.

This drudgery can drive a marketer batty. It is tedious, boring, repetitive, time consuming, and hard to do. However, if you keep every sentient being who is involved in the allocation process on the same page, the process will go more smoothly and you will be in a better position than your competitors who don't worry about context. If you don't, your prospects will miss important points about you, your company, your fund, and so on. This is one reason, dearest people of the planet Earth, it takes so long to get an allocation these days!

A typical context-setting session might progress like this:

- This is who we are and why we are here.
- This is who you are and your current mandate.
- This is our fund and how it fits your mandate criteria.
- Here is the executive team's domain experience and years in the field.
- This is a summary of our last meeting. Do you agree?
- The goal of today's meeting is to keep moving toward a relationship.
- Here is the agenda for our meeting today. Is this correct?
- Here is what we hope to accomplish.
- If there's a fit, here is how things work in our company.
- If there's a fit, here's how we understand things work in your company.
- Here's where we're heading next.

This is a simple approach to getting everyone on the same page.

Keep in mind that you are marketing in a dynamic environment. People, specifications, requirements, the market—any one of a hundred things can change that affect the allocation process. Despite it all, you must keep everyone aware of and in agreement on the status. Provide the context for participants in calls and meetings. Establish the context for the players throughout the process. Follow up with status reports to all. Do it constantly. Or else prepare thyself for the weird and the bizarre.

Time Out

OK, before we go any further, there are a few things I want to say about raising funds in general. These things are important, so keep them in mind or you can forget about the fifty-fifty realm.

It's the Fund, Stupid

Marketing a fund that is performing is a lot easier than marketing a non-performing fund. Trying to market stuff that isn't performing to folks who don't really need it is ridiculous. However, while waiting for performance to improve, it is perfectly alright to start building relationships. Investors will respect a marketer who says, "I know you are interested in our kind of strategy, but currently the fund is underperforming. However, we expect improvement in the future, so in the meantime we would like to develop the relationship so when the timing is better, you will know our firm well."

Another thing. Look for a fit. If an investor has a mandate for a private-equity venture-capital start-up strategy, it is a waste of everyone's time to try to convince that investor to allocate to your long/short equities hedge fund strategy. However, if an investor has a mandate for a long/short equities manager who has to have performance metrics of 10 percent or better and an experienced executive team and you are a fit... well, that is good.

Market What You've Got

After you find out what the heck you are marketing, you have to market it. It's that simple. Time and time again, I have seen marketers moaning and groaning about their fund or the market—investors are changing the rules, the management fees are too high, the lock-ups are too long, we have too many competitors, the money is on the sidelines, and on and on.

Stop already. You really need to market what you have on its own merits, which is another good reason to make sure you're marketing something that is good and useful for investors' portfolios. It's also important that it is ready to be shown to investors and performs as advertised from the get-go.

Get on the Road—or on the Phone

If you are a marketer, you must leave the building. The days of incoming inquiries are long gone. Get out of the office. Figure out a way—any way—to get your feet on the road. You will not market anything, ever, sitting around your office. You need to get in front of potential investors if you are going to market your fund. If you find yourself stuck in the office, you are dead meat. Get up off your chair, walk around outside, even talk to people at random. But get the heck out. Marketers who are in the office more than they are out making calls will fail to reach their allocation potential. If this is you, regroup and get your butt out the door. There is not one iota of middle ground here. Once you have things in the works, you need in-house time—but not a lot. The allocation game is won in the field, meeting with investors and developing solid long-term relationships.

I have a theory about the successful fund marketer. The marketer who is the first one into work and the last one out will generate the most allocation dollars. Here's why: a good marketer is up early planning the day and making sure everything is prepared. Then, it's out to the field or on the phone for a call-filled day, spending time at the end of the day on follow-up. That marketer works late, taking care of all action items, and then repeats the process the next day. This is how you spell success in closing allocations, boys and girls. At Brighton House Associates, the sales folk have ten to twenty meetings with prospects a month, every month. Sure, the meetings come in bunches, but they are working to secure their meetings every day, day in and day out. Marketing is a full time job that is as valuable as every other full-time position at your firm. If you doubt this, your fund will be beaten by the competitors who are beefing up their marketing efforts.

Fundraising Is Not for Wimps

Even if you do your job right, the allocation process will rarely be smooth. Be alert, be aware, and don't be afraid to make the tough calls.

Allocations can change at any moment. They can grow, or they can shrink and die. Don't freak out when weird things happen. One thing you must never do is get jumpy and start nodding your noggin, saying yes to things you should be saying no to. Always stay straight, honest, and in control.

As you work with a prospect to understand the current mandate, rarely is it a perfect fit. You may be able to roll out the big guns to overcome an issue or two and to set context. But if a mandate morphs and it's no longer a fit for your fund, say so. Call 'em as you see 'em: "Mr. Investor, I've realized that my fund really isn't a fit for you. I appreciate the time you've spent with us. Here's the company to call. Ask for Bill. Tell him I suggested you call him. He can help you." Your good karma will be rewarded. Everyone appreciates a no-nonsense marketer who doesn't waste time. Don't hide and hope. Face the facts and move on.

The kiss of death can come from nice people wanting to be nice. They agree with everything you say just to be nice. You cannot pass Go. The nice folks are easy to blow on by, but getting by people is not the point of being a good marketer. You want them to buy in, because you know that's the only hope you have of having a happy client. You also know that eventually, you are going to run into the not-so-nice one, and when he or she starts asking all the nice people why they like your fund and doesn't get the right answers, you're toast.

If a prospect says he or she understands your fund but doesn't, the first thing you should do is verify if you are speaking to the right person.

Marketer: "Ms. Prospect, it doesn't sound like you're the person I should be talking to."

Prospect: "I'm not really. I'm just sitting in for Bill who's on vacation."

Marketer: "Perhaps I should call Bill when he's back and set up another meeting."

Prospect: "Yes, that would be a good idea."

Now we're getting somewhere.

Just as likely, however, is that this is the prospect and you have to find a way to help her understand your fund even as she's saying she does. If you move the process along before a prospect understands your fund, it will come back to haunt you. You must make sure that everyone along the way gets it, no matter what. Don't let yourself slip or you could hurt yourself!

The Midpoint

When your allocation process reaches the middle of the in-play stage, you have something that is alive and kicking. Yours to lose is another way of looking at it. At this stage, you are fully engaged and have a 50-percent chance of turning your prospect into a client. The evaluations are in full swing. The relationship and dialogue are good. You've teamed up with the person who is going to get you to the end of the allocation. When your phone is ringing with questions and your calls are being returned, it is truly a great thing.

The Value Propositions

As a marketer, you are continually conveying the value proposition of your fund. But as you head into the fifty-fifty realm, you need to get the potential investor's buy-in to your value propositions or have a clear understanding of what your prospect sees the value propositions to be. When a prospect sees the value, wants the fund, and knows why it's a good thing, the game is getting interesting.

It is precisely at this point that you as a good marketer don't fall all over yourself trying to get the allocation done. You must make sure that the prospect truly understands the value and that he or she is convinced your fund is a fit. Don't assume a potential investor truly understands the value simply because he or she says so. Verify. If you try to close an allocation when the value propositions are not fully understood, you decrease your chances of closing the business.

"So, dear prospect, it seems that you see the value of my fund and a fit. Please take a moment and explain to me what you've learned and why it works for you and your current mandate. It would help me to hear it from your perspective."

Now, it's likely that one of three things will happen. The prospect may echo the value propositions you conveyed. If this happens, bravo! You've done well. The prospect also may cite one or more value propositions that you've never heard before. This is also good. The fact is, IT DOES NOT MATTER WHAT YOU THINK THE VALUE PROPOSITIONS ARE. Your prospect knows what they are for him or her, so listen closely. He or she is giving you a gift: new value props that you can use to pitch other prospects.

However, if the prospect is unable to articulate the value propositions—yours or theirs—either he or she doesn't really understand what they are or you missed something along the way. GO BACK TO SQUARE ONE. It's what you must do. Start the marketing process over, right from the get-go. Take the prospect on the journey that you thought got you to fifty-fifty. Pull up a chair, cancel all your calls, get some coffee, and begin: "So, we started talking to you folks about three months ago . . ."

The Long and Winding Road

After your firm's value propositions have been laid out and bought off on, the prospect might ask for your due diligence questionnaire or private placement memorandum (PPM) and subscription agreement. This is part of the due diligence process. At this point, you and your counterpart are winding your way through each other's corporate gotchas. You have bonded and you both want to get the allocation done. You keep each other well informed and forewarn each other about any unwritten rules—the ones that explain what truly can and can't work at each other's companies. You've set the tone, choreographed the dance, and the process is moving in step. I have been marketing for a VERY long time and for every really good deal I've done, I always have found a navigator on the client side to help me learn how to market to his or her firm.

Never push hard to complete an allocation in a room full of people. At most say your company tries hard to understand investor mandates and meet investor needs. Then stop and say no more. This is a highly regulated industry and everyone knows there are lines that must never be crossed. Never hint or refer to special situations. Not a word. Nada. All discussions should be done with the powers that be on both sides of the table wanting to get to an understanding of what it will take to get an allocation pushed over the line. This also means adhering rigorously to SEC standards and guidelines.

After you discuss the PPM and subscription agreement terms with your counterpart, he or she confirms a date for the allocation of funds and a time line for getting there. As you head toward the end of this stage, it is appropriate for your inside contact to connect you to the person who can give you the nod.

When the time is right, explain that it would be great if you could get in front of or on the line with the decision maker. When you get that call, you are heading into the final stretch—75 percent land.

As part of the allocation process, most investors have a short list of potential funds they have vetted and now the investor is going to figure out who is best for their portfolio. If you take a quick step back and put yourself in the prospect's shoes, they have to have a strategy to get the best manager they can with the most favorable opportunity for making returns on their investment. So, typically, you find that the investment executive who is the recommender or decision maker is courting a few managers to keep everyone on their toes.

Please remember that talking to an investment executive and being told that you have a shot, isn't going to get you to the next level, which is the VERBAL. The verbal is when someone in the know, behind the scenes, or the main person who owns the mandate says to you, "Joe, you and your fund have been chosen for an allocation."

The Battle for Control

During the allocation process, someone has to take control. It is part of the archetypal dynamic of every allocation. Here's a surprise: it doesn't always have to be you! It doesn't matter who is in control of the process or what side of the table he or she is on. What does matter is that the owner of the mandate wants to get the allocation done.

One thing to keep in mind is that you are marketing to make a living. If your boss wants to take the lead, or if someone in the prospect's organization wants to move it forward, it's not a problem. He or she is your new best friend. You don't have to be the sunshine glory marketer; you just have to be the guy or gal who gets the bonus check.

Never Lose Your Sphere of Influence

You may relinquish control of an allocation, but you should never ever give up an opportunity to influence it. Most marketers, however, let opportunities to influence the allocation slip by time after time. Here's a common scenario: A marketer has a meeting with a prospect. At the end, everyone agrees to a follow-up meeting. Someone at the meeting volunteers to organize the next meeting—and the marketer lets them. BLAM! The process just moved out of the marketer's sphere of influence.

A smart marketer doesn't let this happen. He or she sees that the ball is in play and grabs it before anyone else: "Hey, it's my job to move this along. I'll call so and so, get a list of who should be there, schedule it, and write up an agenda." The good marketer realizes that after folks leave the meeting and get involved in their regular work, it's unlikely that setting up the next meeting will be their top priority. If the marketer doesn't step up to the plate, he or she will be stuck waiting on the prospect rather than able to move forward.

You must be vigilant about not letting any chance to exert your influence elude your grasp. I mean absolutely nothing. It is paramount to grab anything and everything that can help you move the process forward. The tiniest, most seemingly insignificant things can halt the movement of an allocation. That is why the marketer has to be aware of everything that's going on. Hey! I'm not a big detail freak. But when an allocation starts to sprout some legs, you better put on your white gloves and pull out your magnifying glass.

Timing Is Everything

And everything is timing. The definition of luck is being in the right place at the right time and knowing what to do.

Here's a joke about timing. A guy jumps off the 120th floor of a building. As he is flying by the 73rd floor, he's says to a fellow on the balcony, "Hey! How am I doing?" to which the fellow replies, "So far, so good!" Bada bing bada boom!

Timing is a strange element of every allocation. It is either a blessing or a curse. As a quarter starts to cycle, allocations inevitably start to move. Sometimes they slip out, in which case they roll over into the next quarter, and sometimes they get hot and need to get done. Often, the sense of timing and urgency is different, person to person. An executive may want to get an allocation done fast, but the person he or she has assigned it to may be overloaded and doesn't have the bandwidth.

The issue here is that waiting for a signed subscription agreement can be its own form of torture. You received the verbal that your firm has been selected for the allocation, and now you're waiting for the agreement to show up, which could takes weeks, months, a quarter, or longer, depending on many variables.

If the timing is within your allocation window then, hey, it's on the plate! If your fund is reaching capacity and the allocation is out many months, then it's off the plate—until the time comes to put it back on. You must monitor the time frame of an allocation. There is nothing worse than getting to the 75 percent mark and having an allocation fall off the table because of bad timing. The net-net: the marketer wrestles with timing 24/7.

When you bring in an allocation and the timing's right, you go from goat to god.

Your Time and Your Pipeline

Use your time wisely. It is a known fact that if you spend a lot of time working your investor targets and converting them to prospects, and you do it right, you will succeed. To ensure your targets and prospects are always top of mind, have a list and the status of each in front of you at all times. I recommend a white board with three columns:

- *Identified.* These are the investors whom you have not spoken with, but who fit your predetermined investor profile.
- *In Play.* These are qualified investors with whom you are beginning or having an ongoing dialogue by phone, e-mail, or in face-to-face meetings.
- *In Process.* These investors are conducting due diligence, asking for information, and monitoring your performance. You have a verbal, and understand the general timing of allocation.

Everyone needs to be the lord and master of his or her list. Most marketers have some sort of list. In some cases, their list is controlled by a CRM (customer relationship management) system or a list management application. In some cases, their list controls them. Ugh!

Please keep in mind that twenty to twenty-five identified prospects will net you eight to ten in-play prospects, which will eventually result in two to three who are in process, depending on a myriad of variables. The point here is that canvassing the market for investor fits is a numbers game.

After you put each investor target or prospect into one of these three categories, write down your next action or task. Then, any time anyone comes into your cube or office, say, "Hey, here's my list and some ideas for getting to the next step. What do you think?" Get everyone's opinion.

Start every day reviewing your list, and either taking action or thinking about what you can do to move each investor target or prospect along. Moving along means up or off the list.

Working through your list can take twenty minutes or all day. After you do all you can, start to work on your secondary list—but only until the end of the day. The next morning, start again at the top with your number one prospect and think about how you can move that process along today. Take whatever action you can, and then move down to number two. When something moves off your list, something on your secondary list gets promoted.

Here's the thing: the first thing most marketers do is spend time on their least important prospects. What's worse is when they wind up spending their entire day on them. They get to 5 p.m. and haven't spent a minute on their top prospects. This makes no sense.

The way to fundraise is to focus on the investor targets and prospects that matter most. Do it first, do it every day. It's an easy formula: first things first, and then on to what's next after that.

It is also a known fact that if you take time to think about what the heck you are doing, raising money gets a whole lot easier. Thinking is time well spent. Tune your Internet radio to the Celtics channel and just sit and think.

Here's a hint: think about your strategies and tactics.

Strategy and Tactics

The bane of marketers is that they don't stop to think. They like to take action. Make things happen.

Earlier I mentioned that developing prospects takes patience. It also takes a strategy. You need to create a profile of who you need to go after. Before approaching investor targets and prospects, devise a game plan. Then, all the while you're in an allocation cycle you should be anticipating the prospect's actions and your reactions, thinking three or four moves ahead.

It's probably obvious by now that a strategy I use often is turning prospects into friends and mentors. I find a way to be useful to prospects, all the while making sure to convey the message that I'm an honest, hard-working fellow who is trying to make a living and can sometimes make them laugh. I have no problem letting prospects teach me about their market or company. I know I'll repay the favor down the road.

Any strategy must include two things: the straightest path to a prospect, and after qualifying him or her, the straightest path to securing an allocation. You should spend a lot of time thinking about these two things, which winds up being the straightest line to allocations.

After you have a strategy, think about the tactics you're going to use to execute your strategy. Tactics have to be married to strategy.

Most marketers spend a lot of time on tactics and none on strategy. They are also not sure when to use strategy and when to use tactics. Here's a tip: when things start ballooning, faulting, or wavering big time, revert to the strategic.

They're Alive!

When allocations are alive and in process, the game's afoot and something's cooking. I have been marketing for a good many years and I can tell you one thing for certain: they are all the same and they are all different. Are we all clear on that? It's the Zen of Marketing. Best we move along now and close some allocations and generate some inflow.

DENNIS FORD *is President and CEO of Brighton House Associates and responsible for the overall business growth of BHA. He has 25 years' experience working primarily with emerging technology companies across multiple industry sectors. Dennis is an expert at using database services to create business solutions and using the Internet to create an interactive dialogue between buyers and sellers. He is a big proponent of using profiling and matching technology to find that all-important "business fit" in the marketing and selling process. He is also an expert in social networking strategies and technology. Dennis is the author of* The Peddler's Prerogative, *a well-received book on selling (www.thepeddlersprerogative.com).*

Nurturing Your Investor Relationships

CHAPTER 10

The Value of Consistent and Appropriate Follow-Up

Glenn Goldstein

You leave a message for a target investor, and you don't get a call back. You meet with a prospect, who says he or she will be in touch, and you don't hear anything. What's a marketer to think?

A great many think the investors are not interested in their funds. Because clearly, if the investors were interested they would have called. Right?

Let me ask you a question: Did you ever forget to return a call? Were you ever too busy to talk? Have you ever taken time to mull something over? And what happens when someone follows up with you down the road?

The fact is, these things happen to all of us and usually we're grateful when someone remembers to call us back. And yet, too often, when we put on our marketing hat and don't hear back from prospects, we assume it's a no, that they're not interested.

It's true that some prospects may not be interested. However, you should not assume that to be the case—at least, not if you want to be successful. Not following up is the biggest mistake marketers make.

The second biggest mistake is following up only once. Just as you place your call, your prospect takes a call on the other line, goes into the next office, or steps out to lunch. But because you've called only once, you've missed your chance.

Consistently persistent. That's what the smart, successful marketers are. They stop following up only if and when prospects say that they are not interested. Even then, they may ask if they should check back at some future date. If prospects say yes, then these marketers find ways to keep those prospects in the proverbial funnel, staying in touch and communicating something of value, until the prospects are ready.

Is this tedious and tiresome? Not to true marketers. They know the value of getting an answer—even if that answer is no. They know that this is what it takes to compete today, and they enjoy the hunt as well as the catch.

Your marketing materials are first rate, your pitch is concise, coherent, and compelling, and your performance is top quartile. So why aren't you raising more capital? It could be that your follow up skills are lacking.

Everything in life is about timing. Raising capital is no different. You must stay in front of the investor, so when the time is right, you are in the position to move through the due diligence process and receive an allocation.

An interesting fact is that 60 percent of all connections occur after the fourth contact. Even more interesting is that most marketers give up after the second or third attempt. Remember, fundraising is one part contact and four parts follow-up. So, your odds of success rely on your ability to be consistently persistent.

Given these facts, why don't more marketers follow up more effectively? There are many reasons:

- They don't want to appear pushy or to "bother the prospect"
- They get distracted, and it slips through the cracks
- They are under the false impression that if prospects are really interested, they will call back

- They are shooting from the hip and have no system in place to follow up

Make no mistake. Investors are busy, and there are a lot of people inside and outside their firms vying for their attention. To be successful, you need to rise above the noise and attract and maintain their attention. To stay on track, you need a follow-up system.

Tools of the Trade

As we've mentioned before, there are three types of people you will be following up with:

- Investors you have identified as prospects but have not yet spoken with
- Prospects who have expressed an interest in your firm, and with whom you have started a dialogue
- Investors who are performing due diligence on your firm, and with whom you are building a relationship

Just as you cannot build a house with only a hammer, you should not rely on just one method of communication when building your follow-up system. Telephone, e-mail, direct mail, and face-to-face communications all have their advantages and should be leveraged accordingly.

Since the investment allocation cycle can be nine to eighteen months or longer, you should plan a series of follow-up actions at different points in the cycle.

Understanding your prospects and where you are with them in the relationship-building cycle can help you better understand the most effective method for follow-up.

Follow-Up During Prospecting

The very first follow-up may actually be following up with a potential investor based upon an initial interest in your strategy. E-mail can be a very efficient tool for this, but beware, investors are inundated with e-mails, so your message needs to be compelling enough to get their attention.

In the subject line, you want to highlight one of your strengths. For example: "Top Quartile Institutional Quality Emerging Markets Manager."

Remember, the purpose of the e-mail is to generate enough attention and interest to get to the next step, a conversation with the investor. You are not using this correspondence to secure an allocation. The information provided should be brief but compelling.

Investors are looking for funds with strong returns and a sound infrastructure, so you should address those points in your e-mail—including the compounded rate of return and Sharpe ratio of the fund you are marketing. In addition to performance figures, include bullet points conveying the quality of your firm.

Investors are very busy. You will get better results if you are proactive in your follow-up. So rather than asking the investor to take action, at the end of the e-mail state that you will follow up with a phone call to discuss further, and then call within 24 to 48 hours of your e-mail.

Follow-Up After the Initial Contact

After you've successfully reached the investor and had your initial conversation, it is likely that he or she will ask you to send some fund information. Too many marketers fulfill the request and then make the common mistake of adding the "interested" investor to the monthly e-mail distribution list. For many funds this is the extent of their follow-up system: A polite e-mail with the monthly tear sheet and a suggestion that if interested, the investor should let you know. So soft, so passive, and so futile!

IF YOU WANT RESULTS, you must stand out from the crowd. Don't be a lemming and follow the pack. That won't get you noticed or remembered.

One simple way to help differentiate yourself is to follow up your conversation with a handwritten thank-you note. Sure, e-mail is easier and quicker, but in today's fast-paced environment, your personalized touch will stand out and not get lost in the investor's inbox.

Undoubtedly the telephone can be a great follow-up tool, since it is quick and inexpensive. However, it can also be extremely frustrating, since so many investors either screen calls or view a call as an interruption and simply allow incoming calls to go to voice mail. So if you choose to follow up by phone, don't get caught off-guard by voice mail. Be prepared to leave a short, to-the-point message. Give a window of time during which the investor can reach you, and let him or her know that you will call again if you don't hear back. For example, "I will be in the office and available for a call today between 4 p.m. and 6 p.m. If I don't hear from you, I will try you again tomorrow at 11:45 a.m."

In a perfect world, the investor would call you back, but unfortunately, we do not live in a perfect world. Scheduling follow-up tasks will create the discipline necessary for consistent follow-up.

Follow-Up After the Meeting

Have you ever found yourself in this situation? You had a great meeting with a potential investor. He or she liked your strategy, was favorably impressed with your performance, and wanted to continue the dialogue. You return to your office feeling good about the whole experience. Then days, weeks, and months go by. You've lobbed a few calls into the "interested" investor, but you can't seem to get any further traction.

Unfortunately, this is all too common. To mitigate this, end every call and every meeting by scheduling the appropriate next steps. Get as specific as possible as to what is to happen next and get buy-in from the investor.

You must understand the decision-making process of your prospective investor in order to know how to follow up appropriately. Different types of investors have different requirements throughout the due diligence process and you need to adapt. Not all investors are the same.

The high net worth investor, for example, can make decisions relatively quickly. Often these individuals rely on friends' introductions and recommendations. Their decision process can be somewhat superficial, particularly if they do not have the appropriate resources to complete the necessary due diligence beyond reviewing the PPM and performance numbers. They often invest based upon someone else's conveyed trust. Even in these post-Madoff days, there are still high net worth investors who take this approach.

As you move up to institutional investors, expect a greater amount of due diligence. Sure, these investors will want to know about the fund, the pedigree of the team, the returns, and the risk profile, but they will also want to become intimately familiar with your infrastructure and will likely conduct thorough operational due diligence.

Whatever the case, the point here is that you must align your follow-up activities with the due diligence process that is each investor is conducting. One size does not fit all.

Maintaining a Dialogue

So how are you going to follow up? If making a call and asking "Are you ready to invest yet?" is the only thing that comes to mind, then you need to rethink your approach. Offering an update on your fund's performance, a new perspective on the marketplace, or a thoughtful insight about their requirements is a better topic for a conversation. Remember, you are building a relationship, not executing a transaction.

Marketing events such as luncheons or dinners are also useful tools to keep potential investors updated on your fund, while providing you with an opportunity to showcase your team.

Understand that your objective during follow-up is to establish trust and instill enough confidence in your firms' capabilities that the investor will move forward and allocate to your fund. The follow-up process is much akin to a professional courtship. Over time the investor will either learn to love you or never invest with you.

For How Long Do You Follow Up?

Raising capital is not an exercise for the impatient. The rule of thumb is usually, the larger the investor, the longer the due diligence process. I know of several managers who have been courting some consultants for well over two years—and this is just to get on their "approved list" so they can begin talking with their investor clients.

Sometimes it may feel that your follow-up is for naught. In evaluating your progress with an investor, it may seem that you are stuck in neutral. Although you haven't gotten a no, you also aren't any closer to a yes than you were on day one.

It's at this point that you may be tempted to give up. You begin to wonder: if your follow-ups don't seem to be getting you to the next step, how long do you continue to pursue the investor?

There are two schools of thought about this, and the answer depends on which you ascribe to and your perspective on the potential opportunity.

Here's a brief anecdote about perspective:

Many years ago, a large American shoe company sent two marketers out to different parts of the Australian outback to see if they could drum up some business among the Aborigines. Sometime later, the company received telegrams from both agents.

The first said, "No business here . . . natives don't wear shoes."

The second one said, "Great opportunity here . . . natives don't wear shoes!"

For those who maintain an eternally glass-half-full viewpoint, then I guess you never stop following up. Although you still need to prioritize your follow-up.

A lot of marketers are reluctant to give up on a prospect. But the reality is that there are only so many hours in a day. We live in a very busy world with many distractions. To be successful in anything, and especially in raising assets, you must remain focused on results-producing activities. One of the most frustrating and biggest production-busting challenges is deciphering who is real from who is not. Let's face it, marketers are optimistic by nature and would like to believe that every prospect is a viable candidate for their fund. Don't fall into this trap. Nothing will slow down your efforts more than wasting time with people who waste your time.

With that said, and remembering that everything in life is about timing, you can keep investors in the loop by placing them on your monthly distribution list and then do a personal follow-up on a less frequent basis, such as quarterly. This will allow you to keep track of them with little effort and provide you with an opportunity to escalate the dialogue should their investment needs change over time. At the same time, and more importantly, it will free up your time to focus on the investors who are moving through your pipeline.

A Good CRM Is Better Than a Great Memory

One of the best uses of a CRM, or customer relationship management system, is as an aid in follow-up. A CRM system allows you the luxury of automating your follow-up system, while archiving important information about prospects.

Organizational skills and attention to detail are very important. Just as with any other data-centric application, the quality of your information will have a huge impact on the value of the system. Remember: garbage in, garbage out.

To get the most out of the system, pay attention to detail. Log your correspondence, outbound and inbound calls, e-mails, and all other communication. Most systems will time- and date-stamp each entry so you have a chronological record of your activities. A good CRM will also allow you to store attachments of files that you have sent to the investor.

Perhaps, one of the more important features of a CRM is task management. When properly implemented, this will keep you moving forward with each prospective investor as he or she moves through your pipeline. Never leave a record without scheduling the next task, whether it's a follow-up call, note, or meeting. By taking a systemized approach to follow-up you can be certain that no one will fall through the cracks.

A Final Word

Although the process of raising capital can certainly feel like a marathon, follow-up is really many short races, one after another.

Stay focused and stay the course. It's a crowded market, but with so many fund marketers content to take a passive approach to fundraising, the opportunity for you to differentiate yourself through effective follow-up is evident. Be persistent, be bold, be courageous, and stay in front of investors so when they are ready to invest, you will be first in line for consideration.

GLENN GOLDSTEIN *is Chief Operating Officer and responsible for managing the day-to-day efforts at Brighton House Associates. He brings more than 20 years of financial and business services industry experience to BHA. Throughout his career, Glenn has been recognized as a top producer, having built and managed successful teams at several well-known financial services institutions including John Hancock, The Hartford, CNA, and ESI. Glenn has a Bachelor of Science degree in Business Administration from Bryant University.*

CHAPTER 11

The Allocation:
Funds Are Bought, Not Sold

Colin Widen

Raising capital in the alternative investment industry is something of an art form. Yes, it takes professional collateral, a proactive marketing effort, and consistent follow-up. But because it is ultimately about building relationships, it also takes intuition or a sixth sense for when to push and when to be patient. Perhaps nowhere in the process is this more evident than in the allocation phase.

You've been courting an investor for months, maybe even for more than a year. You suspect, or are told, that the odds are stacking up in your favor. You're anxious to see this come to fruition. Perhaps you're coming to the end of your fundraising cycle.

It's at this point that many marketers have the inclination to push the process along, get the deal done, and get the subscription document signed. Usually, however, that's the worst thing you can do. Rather, you need to give the investor the time and space he or she needs to step through their process. Rarely is an investor acting alone today. So the best thing you can do is get an understanding of who's involved, the steps they take, their timeline, and then get out of the way.

I have been through the allocation cycle many times, and each one has its own story, but they are all the same in one respect: ultimately, in their own time and way, investors come to a decision. After you

have put your best foot forward, you have to let the investor's inter-
nal decision-making mechanics take over.

There is no need to panic or waste extra effort. In fact, it's time to
move your sights and energy to another investor, for the more investors
you have doing due diligence on your fund, the better.

Before you move on, however, take time to think about how you
got to this stage with this investor. What did the investor like or dislike
about your fund? What questions did he or she ask? Investors tend to
think along similar lines, so it pays to incorporate what you learned
from one due diligence process into the next one.

That said, don't obsess about what may have gone wrong. It will
drive you nuts. There are many aspects of this process that are not
under your control. So, incorporate what you've learned into your
approach, and take comfort in the fact that you made it to the final
round. Then stick the shovel in the ground and keep working.

It is rare for investors to choose a fund in a vacuum. Rather, they conduct a search, winnow their options down to a short list, and then
begin the due diligence process. Investors generally don't spend the
time and resources required for due diligence unless they are seriously
considering investing in a fund.

Investors today approach the due diligence process with more grav-
itas than they did in the past. The financial crisis, the credit crunch,
and numerous scandals have made investors wary—particularly those
at smaller firms.

Before the downturn, the due diligence process at many family
offices and wealth advisory firms was unstructured, informal, and as a
result, pretty quick. To give you an example, some years ago I met with
the principal of a large family office in Geneva. He was an older gent
in a tiny office who wore a rumpled seersucker suit. When I sat in the
visitor's chair, he was partially obscured by a stack of *Financial Times*

newspapers. He seemed on the quiet side, but he asked good questions. It was clear he knew what he wanted to know about my firm and its fund.

After about 25 minutes, he announced he had no more questions and stood up. I took that to mean the meeting was over, so we shook hands and I left. Outside I double-checked my notes. Had I confused this firm with another one? No, I wasn't mistaken; it was a billion-dollar office.

I went on to my other appointments and then flew home. Three days after I returned, I received a fax. It was a subscription agreement for $20 million.

This sort of thing was not uncommon before the financial crisis. Those days are long gone, however. Family offices and other small investors are now adopting the due diligence practices of large investors, such as government pension funds and private banks. And large investors are reevaluating their processes to ensure they are rigorous enough, often adding new procedures, such as background checks on fund manager personnel.

This focus on research is the main reason the due diligence process takes longer than it used to. Combine this with the fact that investors want to monitor the fund's performance, develop a relationship with the executive team, and get to know the portfolio manager, and it's no wonder that what used to take as little as six months may now require as many as eighteen—or longer.

So what does the due diligence process entail? Generally, it begins with the due diligence questionnaire, or DDQ. This is a document, prepared by the fund, that lists the questions most investors have and the fund's responses. The list of questions and the level of detail provided in the answers varies from fund to fund; however, they generally cover the basics. That is, the DDQ should answer the most commonly asked questions about the fund's infrastructure, which includes compliance, administration, and reporting. It should detail which state and federal regulatory agencies a fund is registered with, such as the

SEC or FINRA. And it should provide an overview of the principals and any potential conflicts of interest, such as an ownership interest in a broker-dealer or another fund.

Many managers and marketers fret over the length of the DDQ. I've seen DDQs as short as two pages and as long as fifty. Here's a tip: it should be only as long as necessary to cover 90 percent of investors' questions in a clear and concise fashion. Too short or cryptic, and investors may not perceive you to be forthcoming and delete you from the list of contenders. Too long and wordy, and you may suffer the same fate, albeit for a different reason: investors are looking for managers who can crisply explain the details of their funds.

The DDQ has become a staple of fund marketing materials. It is usually the fund's attorney who guides the preparation of the DDQ, although the principals often determine the depth and breadth. There's no doubt that this is a laborious process, but it is a must. Throughout this book, we talk about putting your best foot forward. Think of this as another opportunity to do just that.

After reviewing the DDQ, if they have not already done so, most investors request an on-site visit as part of their due diligence process. The point is to meet all the folks involved, the investment team as well as the operations folks.

Some investors will make a single visit. For others, one visit is not enough. So be prepared should an investor request multiple meetings. In this case, they usually ask for a meeting that focuses on the investment process and includes the analysts and traders. Then they'll make a separate visit to do an operations review. Here the emphasis will be on fund administration procedures, trade reconciliations, and accounting and audit reporting. Fund charters, prime brokerage agreements, and other documents and manuals may also be reviewed.

Funds lost the trust of their investors during the debacles of 2008. It will not be restored overnight. The best thing you can do during on-site visits is be as open and accommodating as possible with potential investors. These meetings are the first steps toward rebuilding trust.

No matter how thorough the DDQ or on-site visit is, you should anticipate follow-up questions. In fact, it is highly likely that you will receive a request for some bit of information that you do not have at your fingertips. Your best bet is to find it, and find it fast. Sometimes such requests are part tests. Investors often want to see how organized you are and how quickly you can react. It may seem silly, but if you want to stay in the race, get on it.

After all your information is in a prospect's hands, there is not much else to do, which is why we here at Brighton House say that funds are bought, not sold.

The fact is that, ultimately, investors are trying to position your fund and others within their portfolios. They have constructed their portfolios based on some macro outlook and set of assumptions, and they have certain expectations of how their portfolios should perform in various market conditions. So after all the questions are asked and answered, investors sit down and evaluate how your fund fits into the specific scenarios they have in mind.

Some marketers have the misperception that investors "shop" for funds, but nothing could be further from the truth. First, it's impossible. Hedge fund strategies are complex, nuanced, and dependent upon the portfolio manager. Trying to compare them is like trying to compare apples to oranges. Second, it doesn't suit investors' goals, which are also often complex and nuanced.

So all you can do is provide funds with the information they request, including the market conditions under which your fund will see absolute returns, and let them evaluate your fund in terms of their own strategies and models.

Another reason funds are bought and not sold is that investors often are trying to juggle the flow of funds. A redemption from another investment may be nearing or, in the case of a fund of funds, the manager may be expecting investor capital. The timing and the allocation amount rests squarely with investors; there is nothing you can do to influence these decisions.

So it is important that you present your fund and its performance record clearly, explain what investors can expect in various markets, and let the investors decide if you are a fit. If they determine that your fund and others will help them achieve the results they seek, you and they will receive an allocation. If not, well, maybe next time.

Whatever happens, though, stick to your strategy and focus on performing as expected. It is one of the factors that investors give considerable weight to when evaluating managers. I've known investors to stick with funds for this reason, even when they underperformed. In fact, this happened to me some years ago.

After year end, my firm scheduled a review with a client, a well-respected consultant. We were apprehensive about the meeting. We had made money, but frankly, it had not been a great year. We had a merger arbitrage strategy and we executed it, but it meant that we missed some big opportunities and that hindered our performance.

As the meeting got under way, the client immediately focused on our "underperformance." We talked about how we stayed with our strategy and noted that if they considered the performances of each underlying sector, the overall performance was actually quite good.

It was a tough pitch. Although there were some very bright analysts in the room, they were all riveted on the bottom line. Finally, one of the team leaders came in, looked at our numbers and said, "Great job. You could have easily chased performance." He realized that despite the bottom line, we did well given what we set out to do.

Another factor that can affect investors' decisions is how you react when your fund underperforms. If you can demonstrate that you consistently communicate with investors in good times and in bad, some investors will stick with you rather than redeem their investment.

Waiting to hear from investors can drive even the most patient marketer close to the edge. Knowing the investment cycle of investors can save you much anxiety. For example, family offices generally have access to capital and funds of funds often have inflows daily. As a result, these firms are more opportunistic and make investments frequently—although they can leave just as quickly. Pensions and endowments, on the other hand, typically must have investments approved by a board of directors, which may meet only twice a year. They are not as nimble but make larger, longer-term allocations.

So get a handle on prospects' investment cycles. If you understand whether the wait is six weeks or six months, you'll sleep a lot better at night. You'll also be able to focus on pursuing other potential investors and keeping your pipeline full, which is really the key to securing allocations.

COLIN WIDEN *is Vice President of Business Development at Brighton House Associates. Colin has more than 20 years' experience managing funds, raising capital from institutional investors, and advising funds on operations and business development. He brings in-depth industry knowledge to BHA, having worked at investment banks such as Lehman Brothers and Deutsche Bank, and consulted with hedge funds and funds of funds. As head of business development for BHA, Colin is exploring new uses and channels of distribution for the BHA services. He holds Series 7, 24, and 63 licenses.*

CHAPTER 12

Maintaining a Dialogue with Potential and Existing Clients

Gabriel Berkowitz

Three years ago, Brighton House published its first newsletter. It had a few short articles on investor sentiment and strategy statistics. Twenty-five people read it. Given that we sent it to 20,000 recipients, the response was underwhelming to say the least. Many firms might have abandoned the project right then and there, but we persevered. Today, we send our newsletter to 35,000 recipients and we have over 5,000 readers.

That our readership grew from 25 to 5,000 demonstrates the importance of committing to such an effort and taking the long view. After sending out the first few newsletters, it was clear that we weren't going to reach a sizable audience overnight. However, we believed it was critical to our growth, so we took the necessary steps.

Frequency was the first big commitment: we agreed to publish weekly. Producing a newsletter takes thought, planning, and effort. Producing it weekly requires even more. That everyone at the company got behind the project was critical to meeting this schedule.

Content was the second big commitment: we agreed it would be informative, relevant, and something readers could not get elsewhere, which is easier said than done, particularly in the daily bustle when writing articles is not your primary job. But week after week, the analysts came through, gathering data and researching trends for the newsletter.

A consistent look and feel, as well as format, was the third big commitment: we wanted readers to instantly recognize the newsletter and be able to easily navigate the content, so it was designed to meet our specifications.

Although we have continually made improvements to the newsletter, our consistency in these three areas is the main reason for the growth in our readership. Too often firms send out a newsletter or report sporadically. They produce generic content. They use a template for design. And then they wonder why it isn't helping them.

To succeed requires a real commitment to the effort. Today, we not only publish a newsletter, but also a quarterly report, which is read by our readers and often quoted in other industry publications. It is also cited on popular industry websites, and referenced in many blogs and e-zines that cover the alternatives industry. I expect we'll be launching other publications down the road.

Effectively and continuously communicating with investors and prospects can be the difference between building the buzz and momentum that is critical to raising assets and never getting the traction that is necessary to be a viable contender. One ideal communications vehicle that helps you do both is a newsletter.

During these times when investors and prospects are demanding increased access to and additional information from managers, a professional newsletter is an outbound marketing tool that every fund looking to grow its asset base should consider. Published on a regular schedule, a newsletter can serve as a direct means of communication on an array of topics. Performance numbers, insight into your team's investment decisions, major business developments—there are a host of subjects and a wide range of information that can be of help and interest to your audience. In fact, done right, a newsletter can sometimes be as valuable as a face-to-face meeting with investors and prospects.

Content Is Key

When creating a newsletter for mass distribution, content is key. Investors and prospects are inundated with more information than they have the time or interest to review. Therefore, it is important to not waste their time, and only include relevant content that will inform and educate.

When it comes to newsletters, I am a big believer that education always trumps persuasion. You may think listing accomplishments will grab the attention of your readers; however, in almost every case it causes readers to lose interest. They see this for what it is: patting yourself on the back.

Instead, use your newsletter to explain the firm's thought processes on investments, comment on current industry events, or spotlight a new portfolio manager or other important hire. Articles on such topics are much more likely to be well received.

In addition to publishing informative content, make it fresh. This may seem like a no brainer, but it is something that needs to be mentioned. If you are going to provide performance numbers, make sure they are the most recent ones. If you are giving insight into specific themes or trends that your fund is capitalizing on, make sure you are using current, pertinent examples.

No matter how frequently you publish, putting together a newsletter is work. So it is tempting to take shortcuts and use what you have or can write about off the top of your head because you've done it so many times already. However, if you want your investors and prospects to perceive you as a leader and resource they can depend on, you must expend the effort to compile the latest statistics or research a new trend. Publish fresh content.

As you develop your content, create meaningful ways for readers to interact with the newsletter. The most popular method is to use links, which may be to your website or others. Another is to conduct polls or surveys. Whether you use these or some other devices, it is important to have readers interact with your newsletter because it gives you measurable data.

Most distribution software tracks the number of recipients who open your newsletter. But how many are reading it? Including links is one way to get an idea, for the software can also track every time a reader clicks a link. In addition, you are able to glean readers' interests. If a link to a White Paper on quantitative investing or emerging markets gets a lot of clicks, perhaps that's fodder for your next newsletter or for discussions with clients and prospects.

Perhaps most important is to remember that less is always more with newsletters. The goal of your newsletter should be to keep current and potential investors engaged with your firm and updated on your fund's progress. It is not necessary to a write a ten-page op-ed piece on the outlook of clean energy in rural Taiwan. Rather, focus on presenting clear and concise information about your fund. Then provide those who are interested in more detail the opportunity to get it, which brings me to my next point.

Make the firm, the portfolio manager, and the person responsible for the newsletter all clearly visible to the reader. If the reader cannot quickly identify the fund and who is managing it, then almost all your time and effort have been wasted. Creating a clear point of contact within the firm invites investors and prospects with interest in the fund to follow up. Here's a tip: directing readers to send e-mail to "info@" does not encourage them to contact you.

A final point on newsletter content. It is important that you comply with all relevant regulations. Consult with your legal advisor and include the proper disclosures when and where necessary.

The Design

When creating your newsletter, give sufficient thought to the design. Since it is part of your marketing materials, it should implement your branding. In addition, it should have a flow that is easy to navigate.

After you have something that you are comfortable with and that works for you, stick with it. Don't get into the habit of continuously altering it. Consistency is key. It breeds familiarity, and familiarity breeds comfort. As mentioned earlier, time is one of your readers' most precious assets. Constantly changing your design causes them to waste time trying to find the information they are used to seeing. Additionally, time wasted searching for information is time not spent on absorbing content.

When designing the layout it is important to facilitate scanning. What I mean by that is, make it easy for readers to pick up information quickly. Use graphs, charts, images, captions—elements that quickly convey information.

Finally, plan to insert the newsletter directly into the body of the e-mail. Avoid sending the newsletter as an attachment because more often than not, readers won't bother to open it even though all it takes is an additional mouse click. Additionally, by having the newsletter automatically display in the e-mail window, something might catch their eye and draw them in.

The Distribution

Perhaps the most difficult aspect of publishing a newsletter is also the most crucial to its success: creating, monitoring, and updating the distribution list. It is an arduous and time-consuming task, and to be done effectively requires a firm-wide commitment.

The first step in building out your distribution network is to identify all of your current investors and prospects. Use these names as the foundation of your list. Then, always be looking for ways to expand it. When new prospects are identified, add them to your list. If your firm goes to an industry conference, ask the conference sponsor for a list of all of the attendees and add them to your list. If a teammate has an introductory conference call or a meeting with a potential investor, make sure he or she is included. It takes vigilance to make sure you are capturing all possible names.

Here are a few tips that can help increase readership. First, give your newsletter a name that has less than 50 characters. Some e-mail programs limit the number of characters they display in the subject line, so anything longer may be cut off.

Second, always have the name of your newsletter appear in the subject line followed by a subtitle. Change the subtitle to reflect the specific issue being distributed.

Third, the old adage that timing is everything is true when it comes to distribution. Experiment to find the best time to send out your newsletter. Commonly cited statistics say that it is best to send out e-mails either first thing in the morning or directly after lunch, as those are the two times of the day that people are most likely to catch up on their e-mails. It is important also to account for differences in time zones. If you are in New York and your target list is heavy with prospects in Europe, time your distribution so that your European readers receive it first thing in the morning. With most mass e-mail programs, you can schedule a distribution for a specific day and time—right down to the minute. You can also schedule it hours, days, and even months in advance. So don't fret; there is no need for you to be up distributing your newsletter at 2 a.m.

Fourth, although it is crucial to send your newsletter out to as many investors and prospects as possible, it is also important not to gain a reputation as a spammer. Spamming is uncouth and uncool. It causes immeasurable amounts of damage, and puts a permanent black eye on your brand and identity. In addition, once you get labeled as a spammer, it's a tag that tends to stick.

To avoid being labeled as a spammer, always allow people to opt out. Typically this can be accomplished by putting a link at the bottom of your message that automatically unsubscribes the recipient's e-mail address from the distribution list. Additionally, either send the newsletter from a specific person's e-mail address, or have a specific name attached to the email. That way, if someone isn't jiving to the tune you are spinning, they can let you know they want out, no harm no foul.

In or Out

If you want to use a newsletter to help promote your firm and your fund, it is important to not merely stick a toe in the water. Commit to the project, and then find the tallest diving board you can and jump in head first. By creating timely, meaningful content, offering reasonable amounts of interaction, and publishing your newsletter regularly, you will be able to spread your message to interested investors.

GABRIEL BERKOWITZ is co-editor of the BHA Investor Monitor, a weekly publication that highlights trends in alternative fund investor sentiment, and works closely on the BHA Quarterly Research Report, which analyzes trends in alternative fund investor interest. He also is a Senior Account Executive with Parker Point Capital. In this capacity, he works with fund managers on marketing campaigns aimed at introducing their funds to new investors. Previously, Gabe was a Senior Research Analyst and Manager with Brighton House Associates, where he spoke with investors, serviced fund clients, and supervised a team of Brighton House analysts. Gabe holds Series 7 and 63 licenses.

Using the Web Appropriately

CHAPTER 13

Establishing a Web Presence: Ten Critical Steps

Marc Avila

I had managed the development of more than 200 websites when I first met Dan McDermott, the founder of Brighton House Associates, four years ago. My company, 3 Media Web Solutions, had worked with companies of all sizes, from Fortune 1000 companies to mom-and-pop shops and a great many in between. Our clients were in high-tech, manufacturing, retail, and healthcare among other industries. We had created everything from simple marketing sites to complex e-commerce platforms. So when Dan mentioned that designing websites in the alternative industry would be different, I didn't think much of it. Every company has issues that are unique to its industry or business.

What I learned was that there is a marked difference between websites for the alternative investment industry and almost every other. Most significantly, the design and implementation of the information architecture are largely determined by the rules and regulations of state and federal authorities, such as the SEC and FINRA.

The information architecture is one of the most important aspects of any website development project. For commercial websites, it is usually designed to make most content accessible to visitors. There is very little information—and sometimes none at all—that requires a pass-

word. In the alternatives industry, it is the opposite. Very little content may be read by the general public. Most information must be accessed using a password and then only after visitors are qualified as accredited investors.

This has numerous implications, not the least of which is that much care must be taken in generating the content so it conforms to the rules and regulations and passes the multiple rounds of legal review. And after a site is up and running, it must be carefully maintained.

Today, having a Web presence is a must no matter what business you're in. However, because of increasing regulation and oversight from state and federal authorities, building a hedge fund site is fraught with pitfalls. Violations can result in launch delays or downtime. So it is worthwhile to grasp all that's involved and not underestimate what it takes to have your fund on the Internet.

A Web presence is not essential for hedge fund managers. Many have websites, but many don't. If you are one who wants to see the face of your firm portrayed in a professional, eye-catching, and inviting manner, this chapter discusses ten key steps that will help you accomplish your goal.

Step 1: Make a Plan

The first step in designing a successful website is to gather information and make a plan. Many things need to be taken into consideration when developing a website, so ask yourself a lot of questions. It's the only way to ensure that your website will meet your needs.

For example, What is the purpose of the website? What is your mission? What do you hope to accomplish by building this website? What is legal and what is not? Who is your audience? What kind of information will your existing and prospective clients be looking for? Is there a specific group of potential clients that will help you reach your goals? Asking and answering questions such as these will help you determine the type of hedge fund content to include as well as the design, style, and the types of images and graphic elements.

It is important to know what you are trying to do before you attempt to do it.

Now check out other websites. Start with the ones you use every day. What do you like or dislike about them? Do they look professional? Are they easy to navigate? Can you quickly find important information? Your reactions will likely be the same as most other users.

After you have carefully considered your goals and needs and you have looked at other sites, do a brain dump and develop your site map. A site map is a list of all the main topics and subtopics. Start with the home page and proceed as a visitor would from page to page. Keep it simple; more depth and details will come later. The site map will make clear the content that is needed and will ease the development of a consistent and easy-to-understand navigational system. As you create your site map, keep your visitors in mind. Here is a sample site map for a hedge fund website:

- Home or splash page with login area
- Investor registration page
- Fund information page
- Investment philosophy page
- Management and/or team biography page
- Fund structure page
- Interactive statistical calculation or performance page
- Letters and articles pages
- Marketing materials page
- Legal documents request page
- Contact us page
- Legal disclaimer page

Everyone wants to be master of his or her domain. To do this on the World Wide Web, you first have to give your domain a name. This could be one of the biggest decisions you make. Choosing a great domain name, or uniform resource locator (URL), commands careful consideration as it is the core of your Web address.

Therefore, make a list of possible names for your hedge fund website. Then visit www.godaddy.com. When you search for a domain on this site, it will tell you if the name you've chosen is taken. If you've already chosen a Web-hosting firm (a company with the computing power to host your website), it may offer domain names as part of their basic package and have the ability to determine if the domain name you want is available.

Don't get discouraged if your first choice is not available. Most domain name registrars including Go Daddy will offer alternative suggestions. If you have other ideas for domain names, you can usually search for several at the same time. Try to avoid using acronyms in your domain name even if it means the domain name is a little longer. People generally remember something that is spelled out better than a bunch of letters. Hopefully you will eventually find one that suits your needs.

Why is registering a domain name so important? Because millions of new websites are registered each year, and your potential competitors are snatching up those domain names each and every day. Everyone wants a catchy name, so registering yours ensures that no one else can use it as long as you maintain your registration.

After the domain name, the most important parts of a hedge fund website are the following:

- *Home or Splash Page.* Your home or splash page should include the name of the management company, but not much else. Do not say you are an investment advisor unless you are registered as such in your state of residence or with the SEC. This page should include very minimal information and should not include your phone number or contact information.

- *Investor Registration Page.* The registration page should inform viewers that only accredited investors are allowed to view the fund's information over the Internet and list the qualifications they must meet to be considered accredited. It should also include a questionnaire that asks visitors questions about their financial situation. Their answers will help you determine if they are valid prospective investors, after which you can allow them password access to your website.

- *Login Page.* The login page may be a part of the home or splash page, or it may be separate. Its purpose is to provide current investors, or viewers who have met the qualifications of registration, with access to the site.

- *Password-Protected Content.* All confidential and client information should be password-protected. Even if there are stringent controls in place, never post the fund's offering documents on the non-secured areas of your website. They should be viewed only by the investor they are intended for, and he or she should need a password in order to gain access. Prospective investors are allowed to see the front cover page, but all else must be password-protected—the SEC requires it. In addition, you must password-protect clients' personal identification and account information. You want your clients to enjoy the conveniences of an online brokerage account—such as viewing brokerage account information at any time of day or night, buying and selling securities, and transferring money between accounts—but that information must be tightly secured.

- *Disclaimers.* Your website should have a general disclaimer prepared by your attorney. In addition, all performance information in the password-protected section of your website should have the appropriate disclaimers.

With this in mind and your site map in hand, begin writing your content by deciding what you want to say on each page. This should be a rough draft; don't waste time trying to get the text just so. Writing effective Web copy is a special skill that requires following some specific guidelines. I highly recommend that you hire a professional with Web experience to edit and rewrite your draft so your content is suitable for the Web.

As you write, determine what links, photos, charts, graphs, illustrations, and other visuals you need to convey your message and show who you are. Use only as many images or graphics as you need to make your pages attractive. You don't want to assault your visitors with graphics. That said, as the saying goes, a picture is worth a thousand words. If an image will save a lot of explaining, use it instead of text. When it comes to the Web, less is more. In addition, make sure your images, graphics, and photos are crisp and slick—in other words, professionally done.

Step 2: Choose Between Doing It Yourself or Going with a Pro

Unless you are a programmer or your creative juices are flowing like floodwater, this is not the time to feel adventurous. A successful website requires a clear understanding of website development, which involves writing valid code that complies with current Web standards and maximizes functionality and accessibility. Be brutally honest with yourself when judging your own creative abilities and Web development potential. You can't be a pro at everything. As a fund manager, it is critical to focus on the areas that require your attention. Therefore, I recommend that you seek professional help. Website development help, that is. You will thank yourself later if you hire an established, experienced, and proven pro.

Find a professional developer who has the capability to build a fully compliant site for your fund—a developer who specializes in creating hedge fund websites that adhere to the highest standards of quality and design, offer refined functionality and usability, and are 100 percent compliant with hedge fund legal requirements. Look for logo design, domain name registration, unlimited e-mail accounts, Web hosting, and free tech support. Before you hire someone, ask these questions:

- Do they have experience building business websites?
- Have they built other hedge fund websites?
- Are they aware of SEC and FINRA guidelines for publishing information publicly?

- Can they meet the needs of the plan you carefully laid out in Step 1?
- Will you be working with one designer or passed around to various team members? Personal attention is best.
- Do they have references? If so, call them. If not, move on.
- What's their track record for meeting deadlines?
- Are there examples of their designs already on the Web? If so, carefully review those sites, not just for quality but also for a style that agrees with your own.
- How do they handle support or bugs? After launching a website, inevitably there are problems or technical hiccups. It happens. It's technology. Therefore, this is an important question to ask. Every developer approaches this differently, so pay close attention to how they respond.
- How are they paid for their services? Beware of any who require full payment up front. By the time you realize they're not as good as they seemed, it may be too late to cut your losses.
- How are their verbal communications skills? Do you understand them when they explain what they do and how they do it?
- How are their written communication skills? Did you understand the content on the websites they've built?
- What's their ability to collaborate with clients—with you? Meet with them. What does your gut tell you?
- Does their work ethic meet your standards?

Use the same due diligence you would in hiring a member of your business team. If you wouldn't hire a Web developer for a staff job, don't hire him or her on contract.

Additionally, most Web developers are willing to work with you on an ongoing basis to perform maintenance and update the information on your website. Many offer maintenance packages, basing the rates on how often you anticipate making changes or additions to your website.

If you prefer to perform the content updates and edits yourself, ask the Web developer if he or she will implement a Content Management System (CMS) that gives you this ability. This, of course, presumes you are comfortable updating your own website. Some managers prefer to have control so that they can make updates minutes after deciding to do so. Others prefer to hand off the website entirely to a professional developer so they can focus on the tasks that are more important for them to handle directly.

Step 3: Use the Right Set of Tools

Having the right tools increases efficiency and productivity. Today's investors require and expect a variety of services, including timely and accurate reporting of fund performance. In order for fund managers to effectively manage their business, focus on their customers, and invest, many choose to rely heavily on software and technology.

Putting your business on the Web also requires the right set of tools.

If you choose to hire a professional Web developer, he or she will be able to help you determine what technologies should be implemented and, in most cases, already have all the tools for building your website and taking it live to the biggest market—the world itself. Such tools include:

- Web-hosting software, which requires a powerful computer that can store all your website files and content.

- Hosted Microsoft Exchange Email, a secure e-mail program that has traditionally been used in large technology companies and now is offered to small and medium-size companies through a remotely hosted platform. Exchange also has collaboration tools that let members of your staff share calendars, contacts, and task lists.

- A content management system, which is software that is installed on the website server and integrated into your website. It allows any authenticated user the ability to manage the content on the website from any computer with Internet access. It has a short learning curve.

If you decide to do it yourself, you have made the wrong decision. For the inexperienced, just trying to choose the right tools could take a lot of time, no less installing and learning how to use them. A professional Web developer will be able to decide quickly what tools are required to set up and maintain your website.

Step 4: Keep it Simple

Your website design must be clear, sharp, colorful, informative, secure, and compliant. It must also be easy to understand and easy to use. Avoid flashing images, scrolling text, and blinking lights. They may appear eye-catching, but they can be quite distracting to viewers. Also avoid using too many colors, fonts, styles, and cutesy bells and whistles, and avoid opening new browser windows. They will slow the loading of pages and annoy your viewers.

Rather, build a website that exudes the same level of professionalism that you maintain as a fund manager. Use a simple, straightforward design. Have critical facts, such as contact information, in a visible and prominent location. Your investors may have large sums of money, but they may not be sophisticated when it comes to technology. They shouldn't need a PhD to understand your site. In fact, the more complex your investment methodology, the more you need a website that is easy to use so prospective investors and clients can grasp the concept and details.

Here's another piece of advice: do not design by committee. It is the kiss of death. It prolongs the process and derails all involved from their real jobs. Empower one or two people to make final decisions and keep the site moving forward.

Step 5: Crank up Your Website Traffic

Your website can look like a million bucks, but that doesn't mean a thing if potential investors can't find you. One of the best ways to get your website noticed is by ranking high in search engine results. When investors use search engines, such as Google, Yahoo, and Bing, you want to be high on the list of results.

Making it easy for search engines to find your website is the goal of SEO, or search engine optimization. To optimize your website, your Web pages must contain the keywords and phrases investors will most likely use when they enter search requests into an engine. Your pages must be organized in a way that is most friendly to high-tech seek-and-find services. And your website should have many other websites linking to you, creating what is called "inbound links."

There are two dominant types of search engines:

- *Crawler-based engines,* which determine their rankings by using programs called "spiders" that visit or crawl websites, analyzing their contents and ranking them according to how likely they are to have what users want. Google and Yahoo are examples of crawler-based search engines.

- *Human-powered directories,* which depend on website owners (like yourself) or someone working on their behalf (such as a professional website developer) to manually enter their listings, or enough information, for directory editors to look over the site and write their own reviews. If you don't submit your site to these directories, it won't show up when they're searched.

Something to note: nobody can guarantee you top rankings, much less the top slots on search engines. Some providers may claim to have relationships with, or an inside source at, these companies, so they can get your website to the top. Don't believe it.

The truth is you can't even buy your way to the top, because position is never sold, although you can help your odds by taking advantage of the search engine pay-per-click or pay-for-inclusion options. Search engines will merge this data with their regular results, which may increase your ranking, but high rankings are still not guaranteed.

If you pursue this route, *be extremely careful that you are not using these options to advertise the existence of the fund,* or you may run afoul of SEC and FINRA regulations. Check with your legal resources. The SEC and FINRA have strict guidelines about what is acceptable and what is not when it comes to advertising on the Internet. Research has shown that as long as you are promoting the management company and not a particular fund, you are not in violation.

To achieve the highest level ranking, gain an advantage over your competitors, and generate more traffic and leads, you *must* perform due diligence when writing your content, and choose exactly the right keywords and put them in the right places throughout your website. Many services will handle this for you, and it's another reason to go with a pro rather than do it yourself.

The following are a few SEO best practices:

- Make your URL work for you. Be specific and creative with your domain name. Use one that uniquely identifies your firm and your brand.

- Avoid using "home page" in the title of your home page. Studies show it decreases your Google ranking.

- Create search-friendly page titles that use relevant keywords and are less than 60 characters long.

- Put individual keywords and phrases in the meta tag descriptions, which are built into the code with your design. Each description should be no more than 200 characters long.

- Be dense. That is, use multiple keywords in a coherent, creative, and compelling way on your pages. Make sure your keyword density is never more than 5 percent for pages with a lot of text or 10 percent for pages with little copy. Otherwise, your ranking could nose dive. A useful resource is SEO Chat.com, which has a free keyword density tool (www.seochat.com/seo-tools/keyword-density).

- Avoid spamming; search engines will drop your site if they think you are. Using meta refresh tags, excessively repeating keywords, including invisible text, creating nearly identical pages, or having inappropriate directory categories (that is, having inappropriate and non-product websites, file transfers, newsgroups, and e-mails) are all considered spamming.

- Link every page on your website to the other pages. Search spiders follow those trails to rank your website.

- Simplify navigation by making every page no more than two clicks away from the home page.

The World Wide Web is a very competitive world. To help ensure that potential investors are able to find you, it may behoove you to register with databases, directories, and search engines, and start a blog. As noted earlier, though, first and foremost understand and respect the SEC rules and regulations for hedge fund websites. The rules for maintaining a hedge fund website are different from the standard hedge fund regulations set in place by the SEC, and they are extremely strict and regularly enforced. Make no bones about it—if you break the rules, the SEC can and will shut you down.

Step 6: Proof, Proof, and Proof Again

You're not done until you proof your entire website. Print it out, proofread it, and proofread it again. Then do it a few more times. Whatever you do, don't trust your spell checker. Typos, bad grammar, misspellings, and formatting errors will make you look like an amateur and not the professional you really are.

After you've proofed your site, invite others to do so, or better yet, hire a freelance proofreader. Proofreaders are easy to find on the Web, but be sure to check their references. It shouldn't cost much, and it will be money well spent.

Most important, after you have finalized your website, have your hedge fund attorney review it before going live. The regulators are very sensitive about website solicitations and you could be fined and prosecuted for how your website is designed.

Step 7: Test, Test, Test

Test your website. Use it as if you were an investor. See how it works from a prospect's or client's point of view. Whether you hired a professional or not, you now know how complex developing a website can be. And with every site—even the simplest—there will be bugs. They can't be avoided.

Using a test site (a twin of your website's live server environment that's used for debugging and development), test everything. Do all forms and scripts work? Is the site optimized to be viewed properly in the most recent browser versions and on different platforms? Are there any dead-end pages, or do all pages have a link back to your home page? Are all your pages printable? (Consider a "print this page" function where feasible; it's user-friendly and appreciated by all.) Are all your pages and navigation consistent throughout the site? Do all your links work and go where they're supposed to? As a service to your customers, you may have links to other sites and resources. Don't assume the sites you are linked to are being well maintained. If your prospects or investors encounter a broken link, they will become frustrated and have a poor impression of you.

When you find bugs, track them, and confirm your fixes. Then test it all again. A fix will sometimes cause another problem or a compatibility issue with different browsers. So always test, fix, and test again.

Step 8: Monitor Your Site

Now that you have tested and retested your website, again and again, you are ready to let the world see the face of your business. This is known as "going live." Even though you're now on the Internet, however, there's still work to do.

After you go live, you should monitor your website activity. Pay close attention to your Web analytics tools. These are sophisticated tools that, if used properly, can be invaluable because they let you see and analyze your traffic. They allow you to track how many people are visiting your website, how long they spend on each page, what pages they find interesting, and so on. Smart Web developers know how to interpret this information and suggest changes that help strengthen your marketing initiatives. There are several options for Web analytics. A valuable and free tool is Google Analytics, which can be found at www.google.com/analytics.

Step 9: Keep It Fresh

Remain diligent and keep your website current and fresh. Remember, if investors can't find the information they want on your website, they may find it on another within a matter of seconds, and you have lost an opportunity. One great way to bring visitors back to your website is to constantly offer new content on a regular basis. Here are some suggestions for maintaining your site:

- Constantly optimize your website for the search engines. Otherwise, your website is doomed to fly under the radar, and won't be ranked high by Google, Yahoo, and Bing. Boosting your website's visibility is a very competitive game, and you should assume that other hedge funds are playing hard and are in it to win. Therefore, keep your website current with the latest keywords and phrases.

- Manage your content on a regular basis. Don't allow your website information to become outdated. Investors will notice and your credibility will suffer. As things change, make updates immediately. Remember, the difference between an old-school business and a website business is that the latter has an audience that is worldwide and must operate in real time.

- Promote your website in a big way. Competition among hedge funds is fierce. Your site could be your strategic advantage.

- Test your links frequently. One of the biggest annoyances to a website visitor is a link to nowhere. Make sure your links work properly.

- Keep your performance reports, newsletters, and blogs current. They give investors a reason to continually return to your website, which is always a good thing, as it allows you, using analytics tools, to track what they view, deduce their current interests, and find trends. This will allow you to give them what they want.

Maintaining your website and keeping it well-tuned and effective is a never-ending task. It is recommended that you re-evaluate your website every quarter, or at least every six months.

Step 10: Stay Legal

One of the greatest challenges for managers of alternative investments is dealing with the legal restrictions and compliance issues. I recommend that you constantly obtain legal advice regarding your marketing objectives and potential opportunities. Your website must comply with regulatory restrictions, while it simultaneously delivers your message and reinforces your branding. Whether or not your firm is registered, you must be careful when communicating your capabilities and delivering critical information on a website.

As with many regulated websites, separating information into restricted areas on a tiered basis is an easy way to build in navigation that's compliant. Have your compliance officer or legal advisor review your site map prior to finalizing it and then again after you've drafted the content for each page. One or both should also review the content and design after it has been posted to a development test site and prior to launching. Restrictions governing your firm's investment fund, registration situation, and regulatory status may ultimately influence your site design and content.

Hedge fund websites typically divide content into the following four types:

- *Public Information.* Anyone may view this information. Such content may include a brief overview of the firm, a description of the management team and biographies of key personnel, contact information, and disclosure documents. This section may also include press quotes and other news about the firm.

- *Forms and Prequalification Questionnaire.* By completing these forms, visitors can request access to more detailed information over an encrypted channel. The information gathered is logged securely for audit and compliance purposes, and forwarded to your staff for review.

- *Fund Information.* This information provides historical Net Asset Values and other performance results as well as descriptive details about your funds. Selected items in this section can also be posted in further restricted sub-areas that require additional permission as designated by your firm and as detailed in your site structure. Please note: this secure area of the site requires fresh content whenever the underlying reports and related documents are updated.

- *Secured View of Accounts.* Individual account statements are able to be securely viewed by investors. Often this is implemented as a gateway to your third-party service provider, such as a fund administrator.

For public information, your website should record generic visitor information, such as which pages were visited, how much time was spent on your site, and originating domain, if available.

For other types of information, much more detailed visitor data must be collected to log the activity of individual users. This establishes an audit trail for compliance purposes and is also invaluable marketing information for your firm. Knowing which pages were viewed by each prospect or investor and when is very useful for prospecting and relationship-management objectives. When individuals log in and visit specified areas of the site, it is possible to trigger e-mail alerts to different investor relations managers. However, as always, it is extremely important to seek guidance from your legal counsel to devise an advisable approach for your firm.

The Recap

Establishing a Web presence is essential for any hedge fund manager. It is as necessary as having a distinctive letterhead or carrying a business card, though creating and maintaining a website have their own unique requirements. You will have to choose an appropriate domain name, create a site map that organizes all information that will be on the site, determine site layout and navigation, proofread the content, test the navigation and links, and ensure your site meets all legal requirements. And when you finally "go live" with your site, you're not done. There's the ongoing process of promoting, monitoring, updating, and maintaining the site. Perhaps the most important thing to remember is to acquire the services of a professional website developer who specializes in setting up hedge fund sites. Visitors to your site should feel the same level of professionalism they do when they walk into your office.

MARC AVILA is Chief Technology Officer of Brighton House Associates and responsible for implementing the company's vision and long-term strategy using next-generation technology. As CTO, he also oversees the continued development and evolution of the BHA software platforms and communities.

During the past ten years, as CEO of 3 Media Web Solutions, Marc has managed the development of more than 200 websites for firms of all sizes, including Fortune 1000 companies, in a variety of industries, such as alternative investments, high-tech, manufacturing, retail, and health care. Marc attended Wentworth Institute of Technology in Boston, Massachusetts.

Afterword

Colin Widen

Now that you have walked in a marketer's shoes, you may be feeling a little overwhelmed. It's understandable. Launching and marketing a fund are enormous undertakings. But with a solid strategy, some business savvy, and persistence, it is possible. Here are some of the more salient points to keep in mind as you go forward.

The environment for raising capital in the alternative industry has changed and will continue to do so. The legal landscape is evolving in response to the 2008 liquidity crisis and Madoff's incredible Ponzi scheme. It seems regulators have finally realized that capital knows no boundaries; it will seek a return. Thus, having proper legal guidance as you set up your fund and embark on your marketing campaign is essential.

Starting a hedge fund has never been as costly as it is today. The barriers to entry have risen. To compete in today's investor world, funds need infrastructure and a marketing plan. Too often, managers think that after completing the proper documents and registration procedures and selecting a prime broker, they will be off and running. Fortunately or unfortunately, investors are demanding more before they provide you with their hard-earned money. They want to know that you have an outside administrator, name-brand counsel and auditor, and a sufficient marketing budget. Many managers have recognized this and adapted. Others have been overly frugal and found themselves at a competitive disadvantage. As the old saying goes, you have to spend money to make money.

An important point that we hope you have learned is that fundraising is a firmwide initiative. You cannot send one poor marketer on a few trips by him- or herself and expect to reach your goals. That will not work. From the managing partner on down, everyone has to be engaged in the effort. Everyone also must have the same set of realistic expectations. Raising capital takes more effort and patience than anyone ever expects, so everyone must be onboard.

Before you launch an outbound marketing campaign, take a good hard look at your marketing collateral. Is it up to industry expectations? Your significant other may be a wonderful graphic designer and you may think you know what investors want, but putting together a cogent package of marketing material requires professionals skilled in this area. We have seen collateral from hundreds of funds. About half mangle the message and include far too much detail given their objective, which is to get a meeting. Make this a priority and do not give an investor an excuse to say no based on poor collateral.

Your outreach, whether by phone or e-mail, should leverage as much industry intelligence as possible. There are sources you can tap to augment your database. If they provide you with up-to-date contact information as well as investors' strategy interests, they can be worth the money. Fundraising is hard enough; spend your time talking to investors!

Perhaps the greatest change we have witnessed over the past 18 months is the premium investors are placing on relationships. They want direct access to managers; they don't want to go through third parties. They also want to know in advance how you'll communicate with them—in good times and in bad. Having a solid relationship with your LPs is paramount to building your business. Let them know as much as your strategy allows, and do so on a consistent and frequent basis. Many managers did not communicate with their investors during the liquidity crisis and the months afterward, and the scars of disregard are still there. Investors may have short memories when it comes to performance, but they remember when performance and liquidity procedures come as a complete surprise.

If you have established the appropriate infrastructure, prepared your message and marketing material, and your performance is good, then you are ready to contact prospective investors. It is likely that you will have multiple meetings with an investor before you are put on the short list. Then the due diligence begins. The fact that an investor is performing due diligence on your fund means you beat out many other funds—you did something right!

That said, there are no assurances you will receive an allocation. This process has taken on a forensic-like approach in recent years, so be prepared. At the same time, realize that there are many factors that affect an investor's decision-making process—some of which you are not privy to, and none of which you can control. So be accurate and responsive, get a clear understanding of the investor's decision process and time line, and then continue pursuing other investors. The investor will let you know if he or she will be making a commitment, which is why we at BHA say hedge funds are bought, not sold.

When you receive an allocation from an investor, your work is not finished. It is imperative that you maintain a consistent dialogue with your LPs. Let them know what you are doing and thinking. Remember, they don't want surprises. Additionally, at some point it is likely that they will have disappointing news from another fund. If you have kept them informed and have a strong relationship, you'll be in a better position to receive subsequent allocations.

Also keep in mind that investors talk among themselves more than they have in the past. There are few secrets any more. Though they may not talk about performance openly, the value of great investor relations—and which funds make this a priority—is discussed often. If you have a professional investor relations program, word will get around. Inquiries may not result in new commitments immediately, but they will broaden your database and may lead to allocations at a later date.

The alternative industry is increasingly being driven by institutional investors. New regulations, such as those pending in the EU, are placing more stringent requirements on institutions than ever before. How and where these investors allocate is coming under more scrutiny. This translates into increased due diligence. A particular area of investor focus is the amount of assets a manager is raising. The minimum perceived to be needed to avoid business risk has probably doubled in the past three years.

Higher AUM minimums have increased the amount of infrastructure funds need and the cost as well as the competition for investor dollars. However, sensing an opportunity, seeders, accelerators, and investors of strategic capital have stepped into the void, providing emerging managers with enough capital to mitigate business risk. Clearly, this comes at a cost to the manager, but that tradeoff may get the fund to the next level where it is a viable contender for institutional money. This trend shows no sign of abating in the near future. It will take more capital to play in this next era of hedge fund development.

At the same time, the reflex reaction of investors to the 2008 crisis was to consider only very large hedge funds and hedge fund platforms. Capital inflows to the largest hedge funds strengthened in late 2009 and early 2010. These investment decisions were guided by consultants and investment officers who valued liquidity and name brand more than returns. They also may have been subscribing to the "this won't get me fired" thinking.

The reality is that larger hedge funds usually underperform in trendless markets, such as those of 2010 and potentially 2011. In addition, as investors become increasingly comfortable with the industry outlook, they usually reach for alpha at the margins. Thus, BHA has seen a recent increase in emerging manager mandates. It will take some time, but investors are looking to allocate away from some the larger hedges funds to their nimbler counterparts. It is a labor-intensive search to find smaller managers, but the process has begun. Consultants, capital introductory personnel, and firms such as BHA, which collect investor information, are all confirming this trend. It is a shift that has happened in many investment cycles. So take heart. Build up your infrastructure, prepare your materials, and keep your performance up. The allocations will come!

Brighton House Associates

Brighton House Associates is a research organization focused on the alternative investment community. It was founded to improve the process alternative investment managers used to market their funds to investors. At the time, the current marketing paradigm was *manager* focused, which was inefficient and time consuming. BHA changed this by introducing a marketing process that is *investor* focused.

BHA conducts unbiased interviews with investors and documents their mandates. Alternative investment managers access investors' mandates through BHA's software platform to find investors who are actively looking to invest and who fit their funds' profiles.

BHA services all segments of the alternative investment community, including hedge funds, private equity and real estate funds, and funds of funds. BHA's fund manager clients are located in the Americas, Europe, the Middle East, and Asia, and its research analysts speak with investors in more than 200 countries.

For more information, visit BHA's website, www.brightonhouse-associates.com, or call 508-786-0480.

Parker Point Capital

Parker Point Capital is a registered broker-dealer and wholly owned subsidiary of Brighton House Associates. PPC was founded to assist alternative investment managers create and execute fundraising campaigns. It broke the marketing mold by eliminating success fees and long-term contracts in favor of a fixed-term, three-month subscription service.

PPC uses BHA's research to identify investors who are actively seeking fund managers and to match investors' mandates with managers' fund types and strategies. Then PPC's dedicated marketing professionals create and execute customized marketing campaigns, contacting investors by phone and e-mail to arrange conference calls and road trips. PPC provides managers of hedge funds, private equity and real estate funds, and funds of funds, with a comprehensive service that is designed to increase the effectiveness and efficiency of their marketing process.

For more details, visit PPC's website, www.parkerpointcapital.com, or call 508-281-2249.

Whitehall Financial Data

Whitehall Financial Data offers an online contact database of institutional and private investors worldwide who allocate assets to alternative investments. It is a searchable collection of profiles of investor firms and their employees that includes contact and mandate information. WFD updates this database quarterly so the profiles are always accurate and current.

WFD's database provides more than 16,000 investor profiles. In addition to contact information, profiles report investors' interests, such as the types of funds and strategies, fund size, and track record. The database is grouped into 12 investor categories: consultants, endowments, family offices, foundations, funds of funds, health-care plans, insurance companies, pension plans, private banks, tax-exempt institutions, union plans, and wealth advisors. Of this universe, 40 percent of investors are in North America, 40 percent are in Europe, and 20 percent are located in other regions around the world.

Fund managers who subscribe to WFD's database can access it online or download it directly to their CRM systems. Investor category lists can be purchased individually or bundled together.

For more information, visit WFD's website, www.whitehallfinancialdata.com, or call 508-925-7712.

Breinigsville, PA USA
29 December 2010
252407BV00005B/7/P